Argyll &
Inner Hebrides

Alan Murphy

Credits

Footprint credits
Editor: Nicola Gibbs
Production and layout: Emma Bryers
Maps: Kevin Feeney
Cover: Pepi Bluck

Publisher: Patrick Dawson
Managing Editor: Felicity Laughton
Advertising: Elizabeth Taylor
Sales and marketing: Kirsty Holmes

Photography credits
Front cover: Ttphoto/Shutterstock.com
Back cover: ColorWorld/Shutterstock.com

Printed in Great Britain by CPI Antony Rowe,
Chippenham, Wiltshire

MIX
Paper from
responsible sources
FSC
www.fsc.org   FSC® C013604

Publishing information
Footprint *Focus Argyll & Inner Hebrides*
1st edition
© Footprint Handbooks Ltd
March 2013

ISBN: 978 1 909268 21 0
CIP DATA: A catalogue record for this book
is available from the British Library

® Footprint Handbooks and the Footprint
mark are a registered trademark of
Footprint Handbooks Ltd

Published by Footprint
6 Riverside Court
Lower Bristol Road
Bath BA2 3DZ, UK
T +44 (0)1225 469141
F +44 (0)1225 469461
footprinttravelguides.com

Distributed in the USA by Globe Pequot
Press, Guilford, Connecticut

The content of Footprint *Focus Argyll &
Inner Hebrides* has been taken directly
from Footprint's *Scotland Highlands &
Islands Handbook* which was researched
and written by Alan Murphy.

Contents

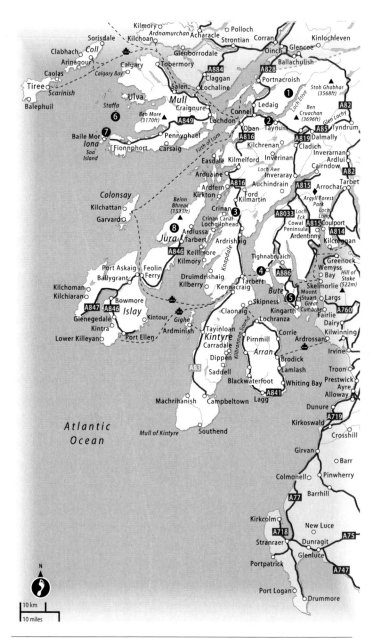

Stretching north from the Mull of Kintyre almost to Glencoe and east to the shores of Loch Lomond, the region of Argyll marks the transition from Lowland to Highland. Argyll may be Highlands-lite to some – less starkly dramatic and more lush – but it has its own special beauty. It's a region of great variety, with all the ingredients of the classic Scottish holiday: peaceful wooded glens, heather-clad mountains full of deer, lovely wee fishing ports, romantic castles and beautiful lochs. Despite its proximity to the massive Glasgow conurbation, Argyll is sparsely populated. The main tourist centre and second largest town, Oban, has only 8000 inhabitants. Oban is also the main ferry port for Argyll's Hebridean islands.

The Inner Hebrides comprise the great swathe of islands lying off the western coast of Argyll, each with its own distinct appeal. The most accessible and most popular is Mull, a short ferry ride from Oban. The variety of scenery on offer is astounding and its capital, Tobermory, is the most attractive port in western Scotland. A stone's throw from Mull is tiny Iona, one of the most important religious sites in Europe, with some divine beaches. Boat trips can be made to the dramatic island of Staffa, looming out of the sea like a great cathedral and the inspiration for Mendelssohn's *Hebrides Overture*. Further west, windswept Coll and Tiree offer miles of unspoilt beaches and great windsurfing and, to the south, Colonsay is a stress-free zone that makes Mull seem hectic. Those who enjoy a good malt whisky should head for Islay, famed for its distilleries, while neighbouring Jura is a wild and beautiful place, perfect for some off-the-beaten-track hiking. If you're after some peace and quiet on Jura then you're in good company, for this is where George Orwell came to write *Nineteen Eighty-Four*. Back on the mainland, the area of Kilmartin is rich in Neolithic and early Christian remains.

Planning your trip

Best time to visit Argyll and the Inner Hebrides

Scotland suffers from notoriously unpredictable weather and that ever-present travelling companion, the midge. The midge is the scourge of many a Scottish holiday: a ferocious, persistent and unbelievably irritating little beast that thrives in damp, humid conditions and will drive you to the edge of sanity. For details on how best to combat this little terror, see page 22.

The only predictable thing about the weather is its unpredictability. You can have blazing sunshine in April, pouring rain in July and a blizzard in May. So, you'll need to be prepared for everything. Climbers and walkers especially must take heed of all weather warnings. In general the weather is milder in summer with average temperatures in July and August of 19°C. The days are longer and public transport runs more frequently, which is handy for getting out to the islands. The down side is that this is when most tourists choose to visit so the whole area is busier and accommodation and transport need to be booked in advance. If you're looking for peace and quiet, spring and autumn are a better option. In May and September everything is still open yet accommodation is slightly cheaper and there are fewer people around. Many tourist facilities close over the winter (late October until Easter), especially on the Hebridean islands of Islay, Jura and the more remote areas of Argyll, and daylight hours are considerably shorter.

Getting to Argyll and the Inner Hebrides

Air
Generally speaking, the cheapest and quickest way to travel to Scotland from outside the UK is by air. Glasgow is the most convenient airport for exploring the Argyll region and there are good links from many European cities, as well as direct flights from North America. Edinburgh airport also has good European connections and there are flights from a few cities to Aberdeen and Inverness. There are no direct flights from North America to Edinburgh; these are usually routed via London or Dublin. There are also daily flights from Ireland and regular flights to most Scottish airports from other parts of the UK. There are no direct flights to Scotland from Australia, New Zealand, South Africa or Japan; you will have to get a connection from London.

From the UK and Ireland There are direct flights to Scotland's four main airports – Glasgow, Edinburgh, Aberdeen and Inverness – almost hourly from London Heathrow, Gatwick, Stansted and Luton airports. There are also daily flights from provincial UK airports and from Dublin. To fly on to the smaller airports, you'll need to change planes, see page 10, for domestic flights. The cheapest flights leave from London Luton or Stansted, plus a few provincial airports, with **Ryanair** and **easyJet**. If you book online, fares can be as little as £5 one-way during promotions (excluding taxes), but usually you can expect to fly for under £70 return if you can be flexible with dates and times. These tickets are often subject to rigid restrictions, but the savings can make the extra effort worthwhile. Cheaper tickets usually have to be bought at least a week in advance and apply to only a few midweek flights. They are also non-refundable, or only partly refundable, and non-transferable. A standard flexible and refundable fare from London to Glasgow or

Don't miss...

Edinburgh will cost at least £150-200 return. The flight from London to Glasgow and Edinburgh is roughly one hour. There are flights to Inverness from London and from many regional UK airports, as well as flights from Glasgow to Port Ellen (Islay) and to Tiree with **Flybe** franchise partner, **Loganair** (www.loganair.co.uk). For full details of flight times and prices contact **Flybe** ① *T0871-700 2000, www.flybe.com*, the local TICs, or **Port Ellen Airport** ① *T01496-302022*, and **Tiree Airport** ① *T01879-220456*. Also visit the **Highlands and Islands Airports** website, www.hial.co.uk.

From the rest of Europe There are direct flights to **Glasgow International** from many European capitals, including Copenhagen, Amsterdam, Paris (Beauvais), Dublin, Frankfurt, Stockholm, Brussels, Milan, Oslo and Barcelona. There are flights to **Edinburgh** from Paris (CDG), Zurich, Amsterdam, Brussels, Copenhagen and Frankfurt; direct flights to **Aberdeen** from Amsterdam, Copenhagen and Stavanger; and to **Inverness** from Amsterdam and Zurich.

From North America Because of the much larger number of flights to London, it is generally cheaper to fly there first and get an onward flight, see above for the best deals. For low season Apex fares, expect to pay around US$500-700 from New York and other East Coast cities, and around US$700-900 from the West Coast. Prices rise to around US$700-1000 from New York, and up to US$1000 from the West Coast in the summer months. Low season Apex fares from Toronto and Montreal cost around CAN$700-900, and from Vancouver around CAN$800-900, rising during the summer. East Coast USA to Glasgow takes around six to seven hours direct. To London it takes seven hours. From the West Coast it takes an additional four hours.

To Glasgow International Continental Airlines and **KLM** fly from New York, **Aer Lingus** and **KLM** fly from Chicago and **Air Canada** from Toronto.

Airport information Glasgow International ① *T0844-481 5555*, is 8 miles west of the city, at junction 28 on the M8. It handles domestic and international flights. Terminal facilities include car hire, bank ATMs, currency exchange, left luggage, tourist information (T0141-848 4440), and shops, restaurants and bars. For all public transport information T0871-200 2233. For details of facilities and amenities at all Highlands and Islands airports, visit www.hial.co.uk.

Rail

There are fast and frequent rail services from London and other main towns and cities in England to Glasgow, Edinburgh, Aberdeen and Inverness. Journey time from London is about 4½ hours to Edinburgh, five hours to Glasgow, seven hours to Aberdeen and eight hours to Inverness. Two companies operate direct services from London to Scotland: **National Express** trains leave from King's Cross and run up the east coast to Edinburgh, Aberdeen and Inverness, and **Virgin** trains leave from Euston and run up the west coast to Glasgow. **ScotRail** operates the *Caledonian Sleeper* service if you wish to travel overnight from London Euston to Aberdeen, Edinburgh, Glasgow, Inverness and Fort William. This runs nightly from Sunday to Friday. Fare start from £59 per person. For more information, see www.scotrail.co.uk or the excellent www.seat61.com.

There are plenty of buses and trains from Glasgow and Fort William to Oban. For details of bus connections, contact **Scottish Citylink** ① *T08705-505050*, or the **Oban Tourist Information Centre** (TIC) ① *T01631-563122*. Bus, train and ferry times can be found in Argyll and Bute Council's free *Area Transport Guides* to Lorn, Mull and Islay and Jura, available at Oban TIC.

Eurostar ① *T08705-186186 (+44-123-361 7575)*, www.eurostar.com, operates high-speed trains through the Channel Tunnel to London St Pancras International from Paris (2½ hours), Brussels (two hours) and Lille (1½ hours). You then have to change trains, and stations, for the onward journey north to Scotland. If you're driving from continental Europe you could take *Le Shuttle*, which runs 24 hours a day, 365 days a year, and takes you and your car from Calais to Folkestone in 35 to 45 minutes. Standard return fares on *Le Shuttle* range from £98 per car load. Depending on how far in advance you book, or when you travel, cheaper fares are available, call T08705-353535 for bookings.

Enquiries and booking National Rail Enquiries ① *T08457-484950*, www.nationalrail.co.uk, are quick and courteous with information on rail services and fares but not always accurate, so double check. They can't book tickets but will provide you with the relevant telephone number. The website, www.qjump.co.uk, is a bit hit-and-miss but generally fast and efficient, and shows you all the various options on any selected journey, while www.thetrainline. co.uk, also has its idiosyncrasies but shows prices clearly. For advance card bookings, contact **National Express** ① *T08457-484950*, www.nationalexpresseastcoast.com; **ScotRail**, ① *T08457-550033*, www.scotrail.co.uk; and **Virgin** ① *T08457-222333*, www.virgintrains.co.uk.

Fares To describe the system of rail ticket pricing as complicated is a huge understatement and impossible to explain here. There are many and various discounted fares, but restrictions are often prohibitive, which explains the long queues and delays at ticket counters in railway stations. The cheapest ticket is an Advance ticket or Value Advance (**Virgin**), which must be booked in advance (obviously), though this is not available on all journeys. A **GNER** London–Edinburgh Advance Single costs between £14-100. Advance Singles with **ScotRail** on this route start from £39.50 for direct trains. All discount tickets should be booked as quickly as possible as they are often sold out weeks, or even months, in advance. A *Caledonian Sleeper* 'Bargain Berth' single ticket from London to Edinburgh or Glasgow costs from £19; to book visit www.travelpass.buytickets.scotrail.co.uk.

Railcards There are a variety of railcards which give discounts on fares for certain groups. Cards are valid for one year and most are available from main stations. You need two passport photos and proof of age or status.

Young Person's Railcard ⓘ *www.16-25railcard.co.uk*. For those aged 16-25 or full-time students aged 26+ in the UK. Costs £26 for one year and gives 33% discount on most train tickets and some other services.

Senior Citizen's Railcard ⓘ *www.senior-railcard.co.uk*. For those aged over 60. Same price and discounts as above.

Disabled Person's Railcard ⓘ *Disabled Person's Railcard Office, PO Box 163, Newcastle-upon-Tyne, NE12 8WX, www.disabledpersons-railcard.co.uk*. Costs £18 and gives 33% discount to a disabled person and one other. Pick up an application form from stations. It may take up to 21 days to process, so apply in advance online.

Family Railcard: Costs £26 and gives 33% discount on most tickets for up to four adults travelling together, and 60% discount for up to four children.

Road

Bus/coach Road links to Scotland are excellent, and a number of companies offer express coach services day and night. This is the cheapest form of travel to Scotland. The main operator between England and Scotland is **National Express** ⓘ *T08717-818178, www. nationalexpress.com*. There are direct buses from most British cities to Edinburgh, Glasgow, Aberdeen and Inverness. Tickets can be bought at bus stations or from a huge number of agents throughout the country. Fares from London to Glasgow and Edinburgh with **National Express** start at around £25 return for a Funfare return (online discount fare). Fares to Aberdeen and Inverness are a little higher. The London to Glasgow/Edinburgh journey takes around eight hours, while it takes around 11 to 12 hours for the trip to Aberdeen and Inverness. From Manchester to Glasgow takes around 6½ hours.

Car There are two main routes to Scotland from the south. In the east the A1 runs to Edinburgh and in the west the M6 and A74(M) runs to Glasgow. The journey north from London to either city takes around eight to 10 hours. The A74(M) route to Glasgow is dual carriageway all the way. A slower and more scenic route is to head off the A1 and take the A68 through the Borders to Edinburgh. There's an Autoshuttle Express service to transport your car overnight between England and Scotland and vice versa while you travel by rail or air. For further information and reservations, T08705-502309. See also page 10.

Sea P&O Irish Sea ⓘ *T0871-664 2020, www.poferries.com*, has several crossings daily from Larne to Cairnryan (one hour), and from Larne to Troon (two hours). Fares are from £79 each way for for car and driver. **Stena Line** ⓘ *T0870-570 7070, www.stenaline.co.uk*, runs numerous ferries (three hours) and high-speed catamarans (1½ hours) from Belfast to Stranraer, fares from £79 single for car and driver.

Transport in Argyll and the Inner Hebrides

It is easy to visit the main towns and tourist sights by bus or train, but getting off the beaten track without your own transport requires careful planning and an intimate knowledge of rural bus timetables. Public transport can also be expensive, though there's a whole raft of discount passes and tickets which can save you a lot of money. Hiring a car can work out as a more economical, and certainly more flexible, option, especially for more than two people travelling together. It will also enable you to get off the beaten track and see more of the country. Even if you're driving, however, getting around the remote Highlands and Islands can be a time-consuming business as much of the region is accessed only by a sparse network of tortuous, twisting single-track roads. Be sure to refuel regularly, allow plenty of time for getting around and book ferries in advance during the busy summer season.

Air

The majority of flights are operated by **Flybe/Loganair** ① *T0871-700 2000, www.fly be.com, www.loganair.co.uk*. For information on flight schedules, call the airports listed on page 7, or **British Airways**. The British Airports Authority (BAA) publishes a free *Scheduled Flight Guide*.

Rail

ScotRail operates most train services within Scotland. You can buy train tickets at the stations, from major travel agents, or over the phone with a credit or debit card. For information and advance credit or debit card bookings visit www.scotrail.co.uk. Details of services are given throughout the guide. For busy long-distance routes it's best to reserve a seat. Seat reservations to Edinburgh, Glasgow, Aberdeen or Inverness are included in the price of the ticket when you book in advance. If the ticket office is closed, there's usually a machine on the platform. If this isn't working, you can buy a ticket on the train. Cyclists should note that though train companies have a more relaxed attitude to taking bikes on trains, reservations at a small fee for bikes are still required on some services. Cycles are carried free of charge on ScotRail services, although reservations are required on longer distance routes.

  Eurorail passes are not recognized in Britain, but **ScotRail** offers a couple of worthwhile travel passes. The most flexible is the **Freedom of Scotland Travelpass**, which gives unlimited rail travel within Scotland. It is also valid on all **CalMac** ferries on the west coast, many **Citylink** bus services in the Highlands, some regional buses and offers discounts on some city centre bus tours. The **Highland Rover** allows unlimited rail travel in the Highlands region, plus the West Highland line from Glasgow, and travel between Aberdeen and Aviemore. It also allows free travel on **Citylink** buses between Oban, Fort William and Inverness. Ferry travel between Oban–Mull and Mallaig–Skye is also included on this ticket. The **Central Scotland Rover** allows unlimited travel in the central belt of Scotland from the East Coast, Edinburgh, Stirling and Fife to Glasgow, and also covers unlimited travel on the Glasgow Underground network.

Road

Public transport is steadily improving across much of Argyll, though don't expect the same frequency of bus services as in the main towns. The main bus operators are **Scottish Citylink** ① *T08705-505050, www.citylink.co.uk*, **Bowmans Coaches** ① *T01631-566809, www.bowmanstours.co.uk*, and **Westcoast Motors** ① *www.westcoastmotors.co.uk*. There are a number of discount and flexible tickets available and details of these are given on the **Citylink** website, which is fast and easy to use.

  Many parts of the Highlands and Islands can only be reached by Royal Mail **postbuses**. Admittedly, in recent years many routes have disappeared to be replaced by Dial-a-Bus services. These operate on demand and don't follow a fixed timetable, see www.highland. gov.uk or www.royalmail.com/postbus. However, in places you can still find the friendly, red postbus. These are minibuses that follow postal delivery routes and carry up to 14 fare-paying passengers. They set off early in the morning from the main post office and follow a circuitous route as they deliver and collect mail in the most far-flung places. They are often very slow on the outward morning routes but quicker on the return routes in the afternoons. It can be a slow method of getting around, but you get to see some of the country's most spectacular scenery, and it is useful for walkers and those trying to reach remote hostels or B&Bs. There's a restricted service on Saturdays and none on Sundays.

Car and campervan Travelling with your own private transport is the ideal way to explore the country, particularly the Highlands. This allows you to cover a lot of ground in a short space of time and to reach remote places. The main disadvantages are rising fuel costs (around £1.50 per litre for diesel), traffic congestion and parking, but the latter two are only a problem in the main cities and on the motorways in the Central Belt. Roads in the Highlands and Islands are a lot less busy than those in England, and driving is relatively stress-free, especially on the B-roads and minor roads. In more remote parts of the country, on the islands in particular, many roads are single track, with passing places indicated by a diamond-shaped signpost. These should also be used to allow traffic behind you to overtake. Remember that you may want to take your time to enjoy the stupendous views all around you, but the driver behind may be a local doctor in a hurry. Don't park in passing places. A major driving hazard on single track roads are the huge number of sheep wandering around, blissfully unaware of your presence. When confronted by a flock of sheep, slow down and gently edge your way past. Be particularly careful at night, as many of them sleep by the side of the road (counting cars perhaps). Also keep a sharp lookout for deer, particularly at night.

To drive in Scotland you must have a current **driving licence**. Foreign nationals also need an international **driving permit**, available from state and national motoring organizations for a small fee. Those importing their own vehicle should also have their vehicle registration or ownership document. Make sure you're adequately **insured**. In all of the UK you drive on the left. **Speed limits** are 30 miles per hour (mph) in built-up areas, 70 mph on motorways and dual carriageways, and 60 mph on most other roads.

It's advisable to join one of the main UK motoring organizations during your visit for their 24-hour breakdown assistance. The two main ones in Britain are the **Automobile Association (AA)** ① *T0800-085 2721, www.theaa.com*, and the **Royal Automobile Club (RAC)** ① *T08705-722722, www.rac.co.uk*. One year's membership of the AA starts at £30 and £28 for the RAC. They also provide many other services, including a reciprocal agreement for free assistance with many overseas motoring organizations. Check to see if your organization is included. Both companies can also extend their cover to include Europe. Their emergency numbers are: **AA**, T0800-887766; **RAC**, T0800-828282. You can call these numbers even if you're not a member, but you'll have to a pay a large fee. In remote areas you may have to wait a long time for assistance. Also note that in the Highlands and Islands you may be stranded for ages waiting for spare parts to arrive.

Car hire need not be expensive in Scotland if you shop around for the best deals. **AVIS** offers weekend rates from around £45 and £126 for the week, though whichever operator you choose be wary of high charges for additional mileage. Even without deals you should be able to hire a small car for a week from £150. Local hire companies often offer better deals than the larger multi-nationals, though **easyCar** can offer the best rates, at around £10 per day, if you book in advance and don't push up the charges with high mileage. They are based at Aberdeen, Glasgow, Edinburgh and Inverness airport. Many companies such as **Europcar** offer the flexibility of picking up in Glasgow and leaving in Edinburgh, and vice versa. Most companies prefer payment with a credit card, otherwise you'll have to leave a large deposit (£100 or more). You'll need a full driver's licence (one or two years) and be aged over 21 (23 in some cases).

Alternatively, why not hire your own transport and accommodation at the same time by renting a campervan. Campervans can be rented from a number of companies and it's best to arrange this before arriving as everything gets booked up in the high season (June-August). Inverness based **Highland Camper Vans** ① *www.highlandcampervans.com*, is a good bet with its two-berth 'Adventure Van' starting at around £385 per week and £75 per day, or £525 per week for its four-person touring van.

Hitching As in the rest of the UK, hitching is never entirely safe, and is certainly not advised for anyone travelling alone, particularly women travellers. Those prepared to take the risk should not find it too difficult to get a lift in the Highlands and Islands, where people are far more willing to stop for you. Bear in mind, though, that you will probably have to wait a while even to see a vehicle in some parts.

Sea

Most ferries to the islands and remote peninsulas are run by **CalMac** ① *T0800-066 5000, www.calmac.co.uk*. If you're planning on taking more than a couple of ferries, especially with a car, it may be more economical to buy an **Island Hopscotch** ticket. They can be used on a variety of route combinations and are valid for a month from the date of your first journey. They require advance planning but are better value than buying single tickets. Another excellent option is the **Island Rover** ticket, which is valid for all routes over an eight- or 15-day period. During the peak summer months it's essential to book ferry tickets in advance.

CalMac car and passenger ferries sail to Mull, Islay, Coll, Tiree, Colonsay and Gigha, and passenger-only ferries sail to Iona (and to the Small Isles, see page 92). The departure point for ferries to Mull, Coll, Tiree and Colonsay is Oban. Ferry times change according to the day of the week and time of year. Services listed in the Transport sections for each separate island are for the summer period (March-October). For full details see the *CalMac Explore Guide* or contact **CalMac** ① *T0800-066 5000, www.calmac.co.uk*. The departure point for ferries to Islay (and on to Jura), and some ferries to Colonsay, is Kennacraig. ➡ *See the Transport sections: Mull, page 77; Coll, Tiree and Colonsay page 82; Islay and Jura, page 91.*

Tourist information

There are TICs in Oban, Craignure, Tobermory (Mull) and Bowmore (Islay). Oban TIC has information on all the islands covered in this chapter. Most of this chapter is covered by the **Argyll the Isles, Loch Lomond, Stirling & Trossachs Tourist Board** ① *www. visitscottishheartlands.com*. The main offices, which are open all year round, are in Oban, Inveraray, Dunoon, Rothesay and Campbeltown. There are seasonal offices in Lochgilphead, Tarbert, Ardgarten and Helensburgh. The island of Arran is covered by **Ayrshire & Arran Tourist Board** ① *T0845-225 5121, www.ayrshire-arran.com*.

Where to stay in Argyll and the Inner Hebrides

Staying in the Highlands and Islands of Scotland can mean anything from being pampered to within an inch of your life in a baronial mansion to roughing it in a tiny island bothy with no electricity. If you have the money, then the sky is very much the limit in terms of sheer splendour and excess. We have listed many of the top class establishments in this book, with a bias towards those that offer that little bit extra in terms of character. Those spending less may have to forego the four-posters and Egyptian cotton sheets but there are still many good-value small hotels and guesthouses with that essential wow factor – especially when it comes to the views. At the bottom end of the scale, there are also some excellent hostels in some pretty special locations.

We have tried to give as broad a selection as possible to cater for all tastes and budgets but if you can't find what you're after, or if someone else has beaten you to the draw, then the tourist information centres (TICs) will help find accommodation for you. They can recommend a place within your particular budget and give you the number to phone up and book yourself, or will book a room for you. Some offices charge a small fee (usually £1) for booking a room, while others ask you to pay a deposit of 10% which is deducted from your first night's bill. Details of town and city TICs are given throughout the guide. There are also several websites that you can browse and book accommodation. Try www. visitscotland.com, www.scottishaccommodationindex.com, www.aboutscotland.com, www.scotland200.com and www.assc.co.uk.

Accommodation in Scotland will be your greatest expense, particularly if you are travelling on your own. Single rooms are in short supply and many places are reluctant to let a double room to one person, even when they're not busy. Single rooms are usually more than the cost per person for a double room and in some cases cost the same as two people sharing a double room.

Hotels, guesthouses and B&Bs

Area tourist boards publish accommodation lists that include campsites, hostels, self-catering accommodation and **VisitScotland**-approved hotels, guesthouses and bed and breakfasts (B&Bs). Places participating in the VisitScotland system will have a plaque displayed outside which shows their grading, determined by a number of stars ranging from one to five. These reflect the level of facilities, as well as the quality of hospitality and service. However, do not assume that a B&B, guesthouse or hotel is no good because it is not listed by the tourist board. They simply don't want to pay to be included in the system, and some of them may offer better value. If you'd like to stay in a Scottish castle as a paying guest of the owner, contact **Scotts Castle Holidays** ① *T01208-821341, www.scottscastles.com.*

Hotels At the top end of the scale there are some fabulously luxurious hotels, often in spectacular locations. Many of them are converted baronial mansions or castles, and offer a chance to enjoy a taste of aristocratic grandeur and style. At the lower end of the scale, there is often little to choose between cheaper hotels and guesthouses or B&Bs. The latter often offer higher standards of comfort and a more personal service, but many smaller hotels are really just guesthouses, and are often family-run and every bit as friendly. Note that some hotels, especially in town centres or in fishing ports, may also be rather noisy, as the bar can often be the social hub. Rooms in most mid-range to expensive hotels almost always have bathrooms en suite. Many upmarket hotels offer excellent room-only deals in the low season. An efficient last-minute hotel booking service is www.laterooms.com,

Price codes

Where to stay

££££ £160 and over   **£££** £90-160

££ £50-90   **£** under £50

Prices quoted are for a double room in high season.

Restaurants

£££ over £30   **££** £15-30   **£** under £15

Prices quoted are for a two-course meal excluding drink or service charge.

which specializes in weekend breaks. Also note that many hotels offer cheaper rates for online booking through agencies such as www.lastminute.com.

Guesthouses Guesthouses are often large, converted family homes with up to five or six rooms. They tend to be slightly more expensive than B&Bs, charging between £30 and £50 per person per night, and though they are often less personal, usually provide better facilities, such as en suite bathroom, colour TV in each room and private parking. In many instances they are more like small budget hotels. Many guesthouses offer evening meals, though this may have to be requested in advance.

Bed and breakfasts (B&Bs) B&Bs provide the cheapest private accommodation. At the bottom end of the scale you can get a bedroom in a private house, a shared bathroom and a huge cooked breakfast for around £20-25 per person per night. Small B&Bs may only have one or two rooms to let, so it's important to book in advance during the summer season and on the islands where accommodation options are more limited. More upmarket B&Bs have en suite bathrooms and TVs in each room and usually charge from £25-35 per person per night. In general, B&Bs are more hospitable, informal, friendlier and offer better value than hotels. Many B&B owners are also a great source of local knowledge and can even provide OS maps for local walks. B&Bs in the Outer Hebrides and other remote locations also offer dinner, bed and breakfast, which is useful as eating options are limited, especially on a Sunday.

Some places, especially in ferry ports, charge room-only rates, which are slightly cheaper and allow you to get up in time to catch an early morning ferry. However, this means that you miss out on a huge cooked breakfast. If you're travelling on a tight budget, you can eat as much as you can at breakfast time and save on lunch as you won't need to eat again until evening. This is particularly useful if you're heading into the hills, as you won't have to carry so much food. Many B&B owners will even make up a packed lunch for you at a small extra cost.

Hostels

For those travelling on a tight budget, there is a large network of hostels offering cheap accommodation. These are also popular centres for backpackers and provide a great opportunity for meeting fellow travellers. Hostels have kitchen facilities for self-catering, and some include a continental breakfast in the price or provide cheap breakfasts and evening meals. Advance booking is recommended at all times, particularly from May to September and on public holidays, and a credit card is often useful.

Pitch a tent on the wild side

The Land Reform (Scotland) Act 2003, which together with the Scottish Access Code came into effect in February 2005, ensures Scotland offers walkers, canoeists, cyclists and campers some of the most liberal land access laws in Europe. Technically it means you have the 'right to roam' almost anywhere, although the emphasis is on 'responsible access' (see www.outdooraccess-scotland.com).

Scottish Youth Hostel Association (SYHA) The **Scottish Youth Hostel Association (SYHA)** ① *7 Glebe Cres, Stirling, T01786-891400, www.syha.org.uk*, is separate from the YHA in England and Wales. It has a network of over 60 hostels, which are often better and cheaper than those in other countries. They offer bunk-bed accommodation in single-sex dormitories or smaller rooms, kitchen and laundry facilities. The average cost is £10-20 per person per night. Though some rural hostels are still strict on discipline and impose a 2300 curfew, those in larger towns and cities tend to be more relaxed and doors are closed as late as 0200. Some larger hostels provide breakfasts for around £2.50 and three-course evening meals for £4-5. For all EU residents, adult membership costs £10, and can be obtained at the SYHA National Office, or at the first SYHA hostel you stay at. SYHA membership gives automatic membership of Hostelling International (HI). The SYHA produces a handbook (free with membership) giving details of all their youth hostels, including transport links. This can be useful as some hostels are difficult to get to without your own transport. You should always phone ahead, as many hostels are closed during the day and phone numbers are listed in this guide. Many hostels are closed during the winter, details are given in the SYHA Handbook. Youth hostel members are entitled to various discounts, including 20% off Edinburgh bus tours, 20% off Scottish Citylink tickets and 33% off the Orkney Bus (Inverness–Kirkwall).

Independent hostels Details of most independent hostels (or 'bunkhouses') can be found in the annual *Independent Hostel Guide*, www.independenthostelguide.com. The Independent Backpackers Hostels of Scotland is an association of nearly 100 independent hostels/bunkhouses throughout Scotland. This association has a programme of inspection and lists members in their free *'Blue Guide'*. Independent hostels tend to be more laid-back, with fewer rules and no curfew, and no membership is required. They all have dormitories, hot showers and self-catering kitchens. Some include continental breakfast, or provide cheap breakfasts. All these hostels are listed on their excellent website, www.hostel-scotland.co.uk.

Campsites and self-catering

Campsites There are hundreds of campsites around Scotland. They are mostly geared to caravans, and vary greatly in quality and level of facilities. The most expensive sites, which charge up to £15 to pitch a tent, are usually well-equipped. Sites are usually only open from April to October. If you plan to do a lot of camping, you should check out www.scottish camping.com, which is the most comprehensive service with over 500 sites, many with pictures and reviews from punters. North Americans planning on camping should invest in an international camping carnet, which is available from home motoring organizations, or from **Family Campers and RVers (FCRV)** ① *4804 Transit Rd, Building 2, Depew, NY 14043, T1-800-245 9755, www.fcrv.org*. It gives you discounts at member sites.

Self-catering One of the most cost-effective ways to holiday in the Highlands and Islands is to hire a cottage with a group of friends. There are lots of different types of accommodation to choose from, to suit all budgets, ranging from luxury lodges, castles and lighthouses to basic bothies with no electricity. The minimum stay is usually one week in the summer peak season, though many offer shorter stays of two, three or four nights, especially outside the peak season. Expect to pay at least £200-400 per week for a two-bedroom cottage in the winter, rising to £400-1000 in the high season, or more if it's a particularly nice place. A good source of self-catering accommodation is the VisitScotland's guide, which lists over 1200 properties and is available to buy from any tourist office, but there are also dozens of excellent websites to browse. Amongst the best websites are the following: www.cottages-and-castles.co.uk; www.scottish-country-cottages.co.uk; www.cottages4you.co.uk; www.ruralretreats.co.uk; and www.assc.co.uk. If you want to tickle a trout or feed a pet lamb, www.farmstay.co.uk offer over a thousand good value rural places to stay around the UK, all clearly listed on a clickable map.

The **National Trust for Scotland** ⓘ *28 Charlotte Sq, Edinburgh, T0844-493 2100, www.nts.org.uk*, owns many historic properties which are available for self-catering holidays, sleeping between two and 15 people. Prices start at around £300 per week in high season rising to £1000 for the top of the range lodges.

Food and drink in Argyll and the Inner Hebrides

While Scotland's national drink is loved the world over, Scottish cooking hasn't exactly had good press over the years. This is perhaps not too surprising, as the national dish, haggis, consists of a stomach stuffed with diced innards and served with mashed tatties (potatoes) and *neeps* (turnips). Not a great start. And things got even worse when the Scots discovered the notorious deep-fried Mars bar.

However, Scottish cuisine has undergone a dramatic transformation in the last decade and Scotland now boasts some of the most talented chefs, creating some of the best food in Britain. The heart of Scottish cooking is local produce, which includes the finest fish, shellfish, game, lamb, beef and vegetables, and a vast selection of traditionally made cheeses. What makes Scottish cooking so special is ready access to these foods. What could be better than enjoying an aperitif whilst watching your dinner being delivered by a local fisherman, knowing that an hour later you'll be enjoying the most delicious seafood?

Modern Scottish cuisine is now a feature of many of the top restaurants in the country. This generally means the use of local ingredients with foreign-influenced culinary styles, in particular French. International cuisine is also now a major feature on menus all over the country, influenced by the rise of Indian and Chinese restaurants in recent decades. In fact, so prevalent are exotic Asian and Oriental flavours that curry has now replaced fish and chips (fish supper) as the nation's favourite food.

Food

Fish, meat and game form the base of many of the country's finest dishes. Scottish beef, particularly Aberdeen Angus, is the most famous in the world. This will, or should, usually be hung for at least four weeks and sliced thick. Game is also a regular feature of Scottish menus, though it can be expensive, especially venison (deer), but delicious and low in cholesterol. Pheasant and hare are also tasty, but grouse is, quite frankly, overrated.

Fish and seafood are fresh and plentiful, and if you're travelling around the northwest coast you must not miss the chance to savour local mussels, prawns, oysters, scallops, langoustines, lobster or crab. Salmon is, of course, the most famous of Scottish fish, but you're more likely to be served the fish-farmed variety than 'wild' salmon, which has a more delicate flavour. Trout is also farmed extensively, but the standard of both remains high. Kippers are also a favourite delicacy, the best of which come from Loch Fyne or the Achiltibuie smokery. Proper fish and chips in Scotland are made with haddock; cod is for Sassenachs (the English) and cats.

Haggis has made something of a comeback, and small portions are often served as starters in fashionable restaurants. Haggis is traditionally eaten on Burns Night (25 January) in celebration of the great poet's birthday, when it is piped to the table and then slashed open with a sword at the end of a recital of Robert Burns' *Address to the Haggis*. Other national favourites feature names to relish: **cock-a-leekie** is a soup made from chicken, leeks and prunes; **cullen skink** is a delicious concoction of smoked haddock and potatoes; while at the other end of the scale of appeal is **hugga-muggie**, a Shetland dish using fish's stomach. There's also the delightfully named **crappit heids** (haddock heads stuffed with lobster) and **partan bree** (a soup made form giant crab's claws, cooked with rice). Rather more mundane is the ubiquitous **Scotch broth**, made with mutton stock, vegetables, barley, lentils and split peas, and **stovies**, which is a hearty mash of potato, onion and minced beef.

Waist-expanding puddings or desserts are a very important part of Scottish cooking and often smothered in butterscotch sauce or syrup. There is a huge variety, including **cranachan**, a mouth-watering mix of toasted oatmeal steeped in whisky, cream and fresh raspberries, and **Atholl brose**, a similar confection of oatmeal, whisky and cream.

Eaten before pudding, in the French style, or afterwards, are Scotland's many home-produced cheeses, which have made a successful comeback in the face of mass-produced varieties. Many of the finest cheeses are produced on the islands, especially Arran, Mull, Islay and Orkney. **Caboc** is a creamy soft cheese rolled in oatmeal and is made in the Highlands.

Anyone staying at a hotel, guesthouse or B&B will experience the hearty **Scottish breakfast**, which includes bacon, egg, sausage, 'tattie scone' and black pudding (a type of sausage made with blood), all washed down with copious quantities of tea. Coffee is readily available everywhere, with most places now offering a selection of cappuccinos and café lattes. You may also be served kippers (smoked herring) or porridge, an erstwhile Scottish staple. Made with oatmeal and with the consistency of Italian polenta, it is traditionally eaten with salt, though heretics are offered sugar instead. Oatcakes (oatmeal biscuits) may also be on offer, as well as potato scones, baps (bread rolls) or bannocks (a sort of large oatcake). After such a huge cooked breakfast you probably won't feel like eating again until dinner.

Drink

Beer Beer is the alcoholic drink of choice in Scotland. The most popular type of beer is lager, which is generally brewed in the UK, even when it bears the name of an overseas brand, and is almost always weaker in both strength and character than the lagers in mainland Europe. However, examples of the older and usually darker type of beers, known as ales, are still widely available, and connoisseurs should try some of these as they are far more rewarding. Indeed, the best of them rival Scotland's whiskies as gourmet treats.

Traditionally, Scottish ales were graded by the shilling, an old unit of currency written as /-, according to strength. This system is still widely used by the older established breweries, though many of the newer independents and 'micros' have departed from it. 70/- beers at around 3.5% ABV (alcohol by volume), known as 'heavy', and 80/- beers (4.5% sometimes known as 'export'), are the most popular, while 60/-, 'light' (3-3.5%) is harder to find. Very strong 90/- beers (6.5% + ABV), known as 'wee heavies', are also brewed, mainly for bottling.

Turn water into whisky

Malt whisky is made by first soaking dry barley in tanks of local water for two to three days. Then the barley is spread out on a concrete floor or placed in cylindrical drums and allowed to germinate for between eight and 12 days, after which it is dried in a kiln, heated by a peat fire. Next, the dried malt is ground and mixed with hot water in a huge circular vat called a 'mash tun'. A sugary liquid called 'wort' is then drawn from the porridge-like result and piped into huge containers where living yeast is stirred into the mix in order to convert the sugar in the wort into alcohol. After about 48 hours the 'wash' is transferred to copper pot stills and heated till the alcohol vaporizes and is then condensed by a cooling plant into distilled alcohol which is passed through a second still. Once distilled, the liquid is poured into oak casks and left to age for a minimum of three years, though a good malt will stay casked for at least eight years.

The market is dominated by the giant international brewers: Scottish Courage with its McEwans and Youngers brands; Interbrew with Calders and Carslberg; and Tetley with Tennents lagers. Tennents was the first British brewery to produce a continental-style lager commercially back in the 19th century, and, despite a competitive marketplace, remains a favourite for many Scots.

Much better are the ales from smaller independent breweries. Edinburgh's Caledonian is a world-class brewer producing many excellent beers, including a popular 80/- and a renowned golden hoppy ale, Deuchars IPA. Belhaven, an old, established family brewery in Dunbar, has some superb traditional beers including a malty 80/-, once marketed as the Burgundy of Scotland. Broughton, a microbrewery in the Borders, produces the fruity Greenmantle and an oatmeal stout. Another micro, Harvieston of Clackmannanshire (once an important brewing country) offers a wide and adventurous range of specialities, including Ptarmigan 80/- and a naturally brewed cask lager, Schiehallion. The Heather Ale Company, near Glasgow, has the spicy, unusual Fraoch (pronounced 'Frooch'), which is flavoured with real heather and hops.

Draught beer in pubs and bars is served in pints, or half pints, and you'll pay between £2.50 and £3.50 for a pint (unless you discover a 'Happy Hour' offering good deals on drinks, usually for much more than one hour! Happy hours usually apply in late afternoon or early evening). In many pubs the basic ales are chilled under gas pressure like lagers, but the best ales, such as those from the independents, are 'real ales', still fermenting in the cask and served cool but not chilled (around 12°C) under natural pressure from a handpump, electric pump or air pressure fount. All Scottish beers are traditionally served with a full, creamy head.

Whisky No visit to the Scottish Highlands would be complete without availing oneself of a 'wee dram'. There is no greater pleasure on an inclement evening than enjoying a malt whisky in front of a roaring log fire whilst watching the rain outside pelt down relentlessly. The roots of Scotland's national drink (*uisge beatha*, or 'water of life' in Gaelic) go back to the late 15th century, but it wasn't until the invention of a patent still in the early 19th century that distilling began to develop from small family-run operations to the large manufacturing business it has become today. Now more than 700 million bottles a year are exported, mainly to the United States, France, Japan and Spain.

There are two types of whisky: single malt, made only from malted barley; and grain, which is made from malted barley together with unmalted barley, maize or other cereals, and is faster and cheaper to produce. Most of the popular brands are blends of both types of whisky – usually 60-70% grain to 30-40% malt. These blended whiskies account for over 90% of all sales worldwide, and most of the production of single malts is used to add flavour to a blended whisky. Amongst the best-known brands of blended whisky are Johnnie Walker, Bells, Teachers and Famous Grouse. There's not much between them in terms of flavour and they are usually drunk with a mixer, such as water or soda.

Single malts are a different matter altogether. Each is distinctive and should be drunk neat to appreciate fully its subtle flavours, though some believe that the addition of water helps free the flavours. Single malts vary enormously. Their distinctive flavours and aromas are derived from the peat used for drying, the water used for mashing, the type of oak cask used and the location of the distillery. Single malts fall into four groups: Highland, Lowland, Campbeltown and Islay. There are over 40 distilleries to choose from, most offering guided tours. The majority are located around Speyside, in the northeast. The region's many distilleries include that perennial favourite, Glenfiddich, which is sold in 185 countries. Recommended alternatives are the produce of the beautiful and peaceful Isle of Islay, whose malts are lovingly described in terms of their peaty quality and the produce of the island known as 'Scotland in Miniature', Arran, whose 10-year-old malt, distilled in Lochranza, has won recent international acclaim. Scots tend to favour the 10-year-old Glenmorangie, while the most popular in the USA is The Macallan.

Eating out

There are places to suit every taste and budget. In the large towns and cities you'll find a vast selection of eating places, including Indian, Chinese, Italian and French restaurants, as well as Thai, Japanese, Mexican, Spanish and, of course Scottish, but beyond the main cities, choice is much more limited. More and more restaurants are moving away from national culinary boundaries and offering a wide range of international dishes and flavours, so you'll often find Latin American, Oriental and Pacific Rim dishes all on the same menu. This is particularly the case in the many continental-style bistros, brasseries and café-bars, which now offer a more informal alternative to traditional restaurants. Vegetarians are increasingly well catered for, especially in the large cities, where exclusively vegetarian/vegan restaurants and cafés are often the cheapest places to eat. Outside the cities, vegetarian restaurants are thin on the ground, though better-quality eating places will normally offer a reasonable vegetarian selection.

For a cheap meal, your best bet is a pub, hotel bar or café, where you can have a one-course meal for around £5-7 or less, though don't expect gourmet food. The best value is often at lunchtime, when many restaurants offer three-course set lunches or business lunches for less than £10. You'll need a pretty huge appetite to feel like eating a three-course lunch after your gigantic cooked breakfast, however. Also good value are the pre-theatre dinners offered by many restaurants in the larger towns and cities (you don't need to have a theatre ticket to take advantage). These are usually available from around 1730-1800 until 1900-1930, so you could get away with just a sandwich for lunch. At the other end of the price scale are many excellent restaurants where you can enjoy the finest of Scottish cuisine, often with a continental influence, and these are often found in hotels. You can expect to pay from around £30 a head up to £40 or £50 (excluding drinks) in the very top establishments.

The biggest problem with eating out in Scotland, as in the rest of the UK, is the ludicrously limited serving hours in some pubs and hotels, particularly in remoter locations. These places only serve food during restricted hours, seemingly ignorant of the eating habits of foreign visitors, or those who would prefer a bit more flexibility during their holiday. In small places especially, it can be difficult finding food outside these enforced times. Places that serve food all day till 2100 or later are restaurants, fast-food outlets and the many chic bistros and café-bars, which can be found not only in the main cities but increasingly in smaller towns. The latter often offer very good value and above-average quality fare.

Essentials A-Z

Accident and emergency
For police, fire brigade, ambulance and, in certain areas, mountain rescue or coastguard, T999 or T112.

Disabled travellers
For travellers with disabilities, visiting Scotland independently can be a difficult business. While most theatres, cinemas, libraries and modern tourist attractions are accessible to wheelchairs, tours of many historic buildings and finding accommodation remains problematic. Many large, new hotels do have disabled suites, but far too many B&Bs, guesthouses and smaller hotels remain ill-equipped to accept bookings from people with disabilities. However, through the work of organizations like **Disability Scotland** the Government is being pressed to further improve the Disability Discrimination Act and access to public amenities and transport. As a result, many buses and FirstScotRail's train services now accommodate wheelchair-users whilst city taxis should carry wheelchair ramps.

Wheelchair users, and blind or partially sighted people are automatically given 30-50% discount on train fares, and those with other disabilities are eligible for the Disabled Person's Railcard, which costs £18 per year and gives a third off most tickets. If you will need assistance at a railway station, call FirstScotRail before travelling on T0800-912 2901. There are no discounts on buses.

If you are disabled you should contact the travel officer of your national support organization. They can provide literature or put you in touch with travel agents specializing in tours for the disabled. **VisitScotland** produces a guide, *Accessible Scotland*, for disabled travellers, and many local tourist offices can provide accessibility details for their area. Alternatively call its national booking hotline on T0845-225 5121. A useful website is www.atlholidays.

com, which specializes in organizing holidays for disabled travellers, recommends hotels with good facilities and can also arrange rental cars and taxis.
Useful organizations include:
Capability Scotland, ASCS, 11 Ellersly Rd, Edinburgh EH12 6HY, T0131-313 5510, or Textphone 0131-346 2529, www.capability-scotland.org.uk,
The Holiday Care Service, T0845-124 9974, www.holidaycare.org.uk, www.tourismfor all.org.uk. Both websites are excellent sources of information about travel and for identifying accessible accommodation in the UK.
The Royal Association for Disability and Rehabilitation (RADAR), Unit 12, City Forum, 250 City Rd, London EC1V 8AF, T020-7250 3222, www.radar.org.uk. A good source of advice and information. It produces an annual *National Key Scheme Guide* for gaining access to over 6000 toilet facilities across the UK (£10.70 including P&P).

Electricity
The current in Britain is 240V AC. Plugs have 3 square pins and adapters are widely available.

Embassies and consulates
The **Foreign Office** website, www.fco. gov.uk, has a directory of all British embassies overseas.

Health
No vaccinations are required for entry into Britain. Citizens of EU countries are entitled to free medical treatment at National Health Service (NHS) hospitals on production of a **European Health Insurance Card** (EHIC). For details, see the Department of Health website, www.dh.gov.uk/travellers. Also, Australia, New Zealand and several other non-EU European countries have reciprocal healthcare arrangements with Britain.

Once bitten, twice shy

The major problem facing visitors to the Highlands and Islands of Scotland during the summer months is *Culicoides impunctatus* – or the midge, as it's more commonly known. These tiny flying creatures are savage and merciless in the extreme and hunt in huge packs. Indeed, it is estimated that midges cost the Scottish tourist industry some £286 million in lost revenue. No sooner have you left your B&B for a pleasant evening stroll, than a cloud of these bloodthirsty little devils will descend, getting into your eyes, ears, nose and mouth – and a few places you forgot you even had. The only way to avoid them is to take refuge indoors, or to hide in the nearest loch.

Midges are at their worst in the evening and in damp, shaded or overcast conditions, and between late May and September, but they don't like direct sunlight, heavy rain, smoke and wind. Make sure you're well covered up and wear light-coloured clothing (they're attracted to dark colours). Most effective is a midge net, if you don't mind everyone pointing and laughing at you. Insect repellents have some effect, particularly those with DEET, but those who don't fancy putting chemicals on their skin can try Mozzy Off ① *www.mozzy off. com*, which comprises 100% plant oils, while the Thurso-made Essential Spirit ① *www.essentialspirit.co.uk*, is also made from natural ingredients. A more radical approach is the Midegeater, a trap which emits carbon dioxide to lure the little blighters within range and then sucks them in at high speed. Those who see prevention as the best form of cure can log on to www.midgeforecast.co.uk, an online midge forecast service that gives five-day predictions of midge movements.

If you do get bitten, spare a thought for the gravedigger from Rùm. According to legend, as punishment for not burying a body properly he was stripped naked, tied to a post and left outside with only the midges for company. The poor chap eventually died of the countless bites.

Citizens of other countries will have to pay for all medical services, except accident and emergency care given at Accident and Emergency (A&E) Units at most (but not all) National Health Service hospitals. Health insurance is therefore strongly advised for citizens of non-EU countries.

Pharmacists can dispense only a limited range of drugs without a doctor's prescription. Most are open during normal shop hours, though some are open late, especially in larger towns. Local newspapers will carry lists of which are open late. Doctors' surgeries are usually open from around 0830-0900 till 1730-1800, though times vary. Outside surgery hours you can go to the casualty department of the local hospital for any complaint requiring urgent attention. For the address of the nearest hospital or doctors' surgery, www.nhs24.com. See also individual town and city directories throughout the book for details local medical services.

You should encounter no major problems or irritations during your visit to Scotland. The only exceptions are the risk of hyperthermia if you're walking in the mountains in difficult conditions, and the dreaded midge, see box, above.

Money → *US$1 = £0.65, €1 = £0.85 (Feb 2013).* The British currency is the pound sterling (£), divided into 100 pence (p). Coins come in denominations of 1p, 2p, 5p, 10p, 20p, 50p, £1 and £2. Bank of England banknotes are legal tender in Scotland, in addition to those issued by the Bank of Scotland, Royal Bank of Scotland and Clydesdale Bank. These Scottish banknotes (bills) come in denominations of £5, £10, £20, £50 and £100 and regardless of what you are told by shopkeepers in England the notes are legal tender in the rest of Britain.

Banks

The larger towns and villages have a branch of at least one of the big 4 high street banks – **Bank of Scotland, Royal Bank of Scotland, Clydesdale** and **TSB Scotland**. Bank opening hours are Mon-Fri from 0930 to between 1600 and 1700. Some larger branches may also be open later on Thu and on Sat mornings. In small and remote places, and on some islands, there may be only a mobile bank which runs to a set timetable. This timetable will be available from the local post office.

Banks are usually the best places to change money and cheques. You can withdraw cash from selected banks and ATMs (or cashpoints as they are called in Britain) with your cash and credit card. Though using a debit or credit card is by far the easiest way of keeping in funds, you must check with your bank what the total charges will be; this can be as high as 4-5% in some cases. In more remote parts, and especially on the islands, ATMs are few and far between and it is important to keep a ready supply of cash on you at all times and many guesthouses in the remoter reaches of Scotland will still request payment in cash. Outside the ferry ports on most of the smaller islands, you won't find an ATM. Your bank will give you a list of locations where you can use your card. **Bank of Scotland** and **Royal Bank** take **Lloyds** and **Barclays** cash cards; **Clydesdale** takes **HSBC** and **National Westminster** cards. **Bank of Scotland, Clydesdale** and most building society cashpoints are part of the Link network and accept all affiliated cards. See also Credit cards below. In addition to ATMs, bureaux de change can be used outside banking hours. These can be found in most city centres and also at the main airports and train stations. Note that some charge high commissions for changing cheques. Those

at international airports, however, often charge less than banks and will change pound sterling cheques for free. Avoid changing money or cheques in hotels, as the rates are usually very poor.

Credit cards

Most hotels, shops and restaurants accept the major credit cards such as MasterCard and Visa and, less frequently, Amex, though some places may charge for using them. They may be less useful in more remote rural areas and smaller establishments such as B&Bs, which will often only accept cash or cheques.

Visa card holders can use the **Bank of Scotland, Clydesdale Bank, Royal Bank of Scotland** and **TSB** ATMs; Access/MasterCard holders the Royal Bank and Clydesdale; Amex card holders the Bank of Scotland.

Traveller's cheques

The safest way to carry money is in traveller's cheques. These are available for a small commission from all major banks. **American Express (Amex), Visa** and **Thomas Cook** cheques are widely accepted and are the most commonly issued by banks. You'll normally have to pay commission again when you cash each cheque. This will usually be 1%, or a flat rate. No commission is payable on Amex cheques cashed at Amex offices, www.americanexpress.co/feefree. Make sure you keep a record of the cheque numbers and the cheques you've cashed separate from the cheques themselves, so that you can get a full refund of all uncashed cheques should you lose them. It's best to bring sterling cheques to avoid changing currencies twice. Also note that in Britain traveller's cheques are rarely accepted outside banks or foreign exchange bureaux, so you'll need to cash them in advance and keep a good supply of ready cash.

Money transfers

If you need money urgently, the quickest way to have it sent to you is to have it wired to the nearest bank via **Western Union**, T0800-833 833, www.westernunion.co.uk, or **Money-gram**, T0800-8971 8971. Charges are on a sliding scale; ie it will cost proportionately less to wire out more money. Money can also be wired by **Thomas Cook**, www.thomasexchangeglobal.co.uk, or transferred via a bank draft, but this can take up to a week.

Cost of travelling

The Highlands and Islands of Scotland can be an expensive place to visit, and prices are higher in more remote parts, but there is plenty of budget accommodation available and backpackers will be able to keep their costs down. Petrol is a major expense and won't just cost an arm and a leg but also the limbs of all remaining family members. Expect to pay up to 15p per litre more than in central and southern parts of Scotland and don't pass a fuel station in the Highlands and Islands if short of fuel. Accommodation and restaurant prices also tend to be higher in more popular destinations and during the busy summer months.

The minimum daily budget required, if you're staying in hostels, very cheap B&Bs or camping, cycling or hitching (not recommended), and cooking your own meals, will be around £25-30 per person per day. If you start using public transport and eating out occasionally that will rise to around £35-40. Those staying in slightly more upmarket B&Bs or guesthouses, eating out every evening at pubs or modest restaurants and visiting tourist attractions, such as castles or museums, can expect to pay around £50-60 per day. If you also want to hire a car and use ferries to visit the islands, and eat well, then costs will rise considerably and you'll be looking at least £75-80 per person per day. Single travellers will have to pay more than ½ the cost of a double room in most places, and should budget on spending around 60-70% of what a couple would spend.

Opening hours

Businesses are usually open Mon-Sat 0900-1700. In towns and cities, as well as villages in holiday areas, many shops open on a Sun but they will open later and close earlier. For TIC opening hours, see page 25. Those visiting the Outer Hebrides need to be aware of the strict observance of the Sabbath on those islands.

Post

Most post offices are open Mon-Fri 0900 to 1730 and Sat 0900-1230 or 1300. Smaller sub-post offices are closed for an hour at lunch (1300-1400) and many of them operate out of a shop. Post offices keep the same ½-day closing times as shops.

Stamps can be bought at post offices, but also from vending machines outside, and also at many newsagents. A 1st-class letter weighing up to 100 g to anywhere in the UK costs 60p and should arrive the following day, while 2nd-class letters weighing up to 100 g cost 50p and take between 2-4 days. For more information about Royal Mail postal services, call T08457-740740, or visit www.royalmail.com.

Safety

Incidences of serious crime in Highlands and Islands tend to be the exception rather than the rule and are so rare that they always make front page news. In fact, if someone failed to say 'good morning' – heaven forfend – it would provoke such an outrage that locals would be talking about little else for weeks to come. In most island communities, even sizeable ones such as Tobermory on Mull, people don't even lock their doors at night, and will even leave their car keys still in the lock. The major safety issue when visiting the Highlands and more remote parts relates to the unpredictable weather conditions. Everyone should be aware of the need for caution and proper preparation when walking or climbing in the mountains. For more information on mountain safety, see www.mountaineering-scotland.org.uk/safety.

Telephone → *Country code +44.*
Useful numbers: operator T100; international operator T155; directory enquiries T192; overseas directory enquiries T153.

Most public payphones are operated by **British Telecom (BT)** and can be found in towns and cities, though less so in rural areas. Numbers of public phone booths have declined in recent years due to the advent of the mobile phone, so don't rely on being able to find a payphone wherever you go. BT payphones take either coins (20p, 50p and £1) or phonecards, which are available at newsagents and post offices displaying the BT logo. These cards come in denominations of £2, £3, £5 and £10. Some payphones also accept credit cards.

For most countries (including Europe, USA and Canada) calls are cheapest Mon-Fri between 1800 and 0800 and all day Sat-Sun. For Australia and New Zealand it's cheapest to call from 1430-1930 and from 2400-0700 every day. Area codes are not needed if calling from within the same area. Any number prefixed by 0800 or 0500 is free to the caller; 08457 numbers are charged at local rates and 08705 numbers at the national rate. To call Scotland from overseas, dial 011 from USA and Canada, 0011 from Australia and 00 from New Zealand, followed by 44, then the area code, minus the first zero, then the number. To call overseas from Scotland dial 00 followed by the country code. Country codes include: Australia 61; Ireland 353; New Zealand 64; South Africa 27; USA and Canada 1.

Time
Greenwich Mean Time (GMT) is used from late Oct to late Mar, after which time the clocks go forward an hour to British Summer Time (BST). GMT is 5 hrs ahead of US Eastern Standard Time and 10 hrs behind Australian Eastern Standard Time.

Tipping
Believe it or not, people in Scotland do leave tips. In a restaurant you should leave a tip of 10-15% if you are satisfied with the service. If the bill already includes a service charge, you needn't add a further tip. Tipping is not normal in pubs or bars. Taxi drivers will expect a tip for longer journeys, usually of around 10%; and most hairdressers will also expect a tip. As in most other countries, porters, bellboys and waiters in more up-market hotels rely on tips to supplement their meagre wages.

Tourist information
Tourist Information Centres (TICs) can be found in most Scottish towns. Their addresses, phone numbers and opening hours are listed in the relevant sections of this book. Opening hours vary depending on the time of year, and many of the smaller offices are closed during the winter months. All tourist offices provide information on accommodation, public transport, local attractions and restaurants, as well as selling books, local guides, maps and souvenirs. Many also have free street plans and leaflets describing local walks. They can also book accommodation for you, for a small fee.

Museums, galleries and historic houses
Most of Scotland's tourist attractions, apart from the large museums and art galleries in the main cities, are open only from Easter-Oct. Full details of opening hours and admission charges are given in the relevant sections of this guide.

Over 100 of the country's most prestigious sights, and 75,000 ha of beautiful countryside, are cared for by the **National Trust for Scotland (NTS)**, 26-31 Charlotte Sq, Edinburgh EH2 4ET, T0844-493 2100, www.nts.org.uk. National Trust properties are indicated in this guide as 'NTS', and entry charges and opening hours are given for each property.

Historic Scotland (HS), Longmore House, Salisbury Pl, Edinburgh EH9 1SH, T0131-668 8600, www.historic-scotland.gov.uk, manages more than 330 of Scotland's most important castles, monuments and other historic sites. Historic Scotland properties are indicated as 'HS', and admission charges and opening hours are also given in this guide. Historic Scotland offers an Explorer Pass which allows free entry to 70 of its properties including Edinburgh and Stirling castles. A 3-day pass (can be used over 5 consecutive days) costs £25, concessions £20, family £50, 7-day pass (valid for 14 days) £34, £27, £68. It can save a lot of money, especially in Orkney, where most of the monuments are managed by Historic Scotland.

Many other historic buildings are owned by local authorities, and admission is cheap, or in many cases free. Most fee-paying attractions give a discount or concession for senior citizens, the unemployed, full-time students and children under 16 (those under 5 are admitted free everywhere). Proof of age or status must be shown. Many of Scotland's stately homes are still owned and occupied by the landed gentry, and admission is usually between £4 and £8.

Finding out more

The best way of finding out more information for your trip to Scotland is to contact **VisitScotland** (aka the Scottish Tourist Board), www.visitbritain.com. Alternatively, you can contact **VisitBritain**, the organization that is responsible for tourism throughout the British Isles. Both organizations can provide a wealth of free literature and information such as maps, city guides and accommodation brochures. If particularly interested in ensuring your visit coincides with a major festival or sporting event, it's also worthwhile having a look at **EventScotland**'s website, www. eventscotland.org. Travellers with special needs should also contact Visit Scotland or their nearest VisitBritain office. If you want more detailed information on a particular area, contact the specific tourist boards listed throughout the text.

Visas and immigration

Visa regulations are subject to change, so it is essential to check with your local British embassy, high commission or consulate before leaving home. Citizens of all European countries – except Albania, Bosnia Herzegovina, Kosovo, Macedonia, Moldova, Turkey, Serbia and all former Soviet republics (other than the Baltic states) – require only a passport to enter Britain. Citizens of Australia, Canada, New Zealand, South Africa or the USA can stay for up to 6 months, providing they have a return ticket and sufficient funds to cover their stay. Citizens of most other countries require a visa from the commission or consular office in the country of application.

The **Foreign and Commonwealth Office** (FCO), T0207-270 1500, www.fco.gov.uk, has an excellent website, which provides details of British immigration and visa requirements. Also the Home Office UK Border Agency is responsible for UK immigration matters and its website is a good place to start for anyone hoping visit, work, study or emigrate to the UK. Call the immigration enquiry bureau on T0870-6067 766 or visit www.bia.homeoffice.gov.uk.

For visa extensions also contact the **Home Office UK Border Agency** via the above number or its website. The agency can also be reached at Lunar House, Wellesley Rd, Croydon, London CR9. Citizens of Australia, Canada, New Zealand, South Africa or the USA wishing to stay longer than 6 months will need an Entry Clearance Certificate from the British High Commission in their country. For more details, contact your nearest British embassy, consulate or high commission, or the Foreign and Commonwealth Office in London.

Weights and measures
Imperial and metric systems are both
in use. Distances on roads are measured
in miles and yards, drinks poured in pints
and gills, but generally, the metric system
is used elsewhere.

Volunteering
See www.volunteerscotland.org.uk.
**The British Trust for Conservation
Volunteers**, Sedum House, Mallard Way,
Doncaster DN4 8DB, T01302-388883,
www.btcv.org. Get fit in the 'green gym',
planting hedges, creating wildlife gardens
or improving footpaths.

Earthwatch, 57 Woodstock Rd, Oxford
OX2 6HJ, T01865-318838. Team up with
scientists studying our furry friends.
Jubilee Sailing Trust, Hazel Rd,
Southampton, T023-804 9108, www.jst.org.
uk. Work on deck on an adventure holiday.
National Trust for Scotland, Wemyss
House, 28 Charlotte Sq, Edinburgh EH2 4ET,
T0844-493 2100, www.nts.org.uk. Among
a number of Scotland based charities that
offer volunteering opportunities. You could
find yourself helping restore buildings on
St Kilda or taking part in an archaeological
dig on Loch Lomondside.

Isle of Kerrera → *Phone code 01631.*

Boasting one of the best short (6-mile) coastal walks in the UK, the tranquil Isle of Kerrera lying half a mile offshore and a five-minute **ferry ride** ① *Mon-Sat 0840-1800, Sun 1030-1800, £5 return, children £2.50, bikes 50p*, from Oban, provides the perfect antidote to the bustle of the town. The island supports just 35 inhabitants, walkers or cyclists may spot wild goats, otters, sea eagles and seals or even porpoise offshore. Five minutes' walk south of the welcoming Kerrera bunkhouse and tea room visitors are rewarded with the imposing ruins of Gylen Castle and views across to Mull, the Slate Islands, Lismore and Jura. Built by the MacDougall's in 1587, **Gylen Castle** sits proudly on a clifftop looking down the Firth of Lorn. A mile northwest of the ferry jetty is **Slatrach Bay**, a sandy beach providing a terrific place for a family picnic. There are no shops so arrive with provisions. However, at the **Oban Marina** located at the northeastern end of Kerrera, you'll find the excellent **Waypoint Bar and Grill** ① *T01631-570223*, which in addition to great seafood runs a complimentary ferry boat service for guests dining at the restaurant (boat leaves Oban's North Pier at 1210 and every hour between 1700-2200).

Connel to Oban Sealife Centre → *Phone code 01631.*

Five miles north of Oban an impressive steel cantilever bridge carries the A828 across the mouth of Loch Etive at Connel. It's worth stopping here to see the **Falls of Lora**, a wild tide-race created by the narrow mouth of the sea loch and the reef that spans most of it, thus restricting the flow of water. The result is the impressive rapids, which are best seen from the shore in the village or from halfway across the bridge.

Ten miles north up this road on the shore of Loch Creran and past the turn-off to 16th-century Barcaldine Castle, a most atmospheric B&B option awaits (see Where to stay, page 37). **Oban Sealife Centre** ① *T01631-720386, Apr-Oct daily 1000-1700 (ring for winter opening hours), £12.95, concessions £12 children £10*, is enormous fun. This environmentally friendly facility rescues seals and other aquatic creatures, which are then released back into the wild at the end of the season. Aside from over 30 displays, there's a touch pool, an underwater observatory and a terrific forest adventure trail. Parents can rest their tired feet in the coffee shop. Bus No 405 runs regularly from Oban to the Sealife Centre.

Appin → *Phone code 01631.*

The road runs around Loch Creran and enters the district of Appin, made famous in Robert Louis Stevenson's *Kidnapped*, which was based on the 'Appin Murder' of 'The Red Fox – Campbell of Glenure' – in 1752 for which the prominent Jacobite, James Stewart was tried by a 'kangaroo court' of Campbells and subsequently hung in Ballachulish with his body left to rot for three years. A road turns southwest off the main Fort William road to **Port Appin**, on the western tip of the peninsula, the departure point for the passenger ferry to Lismore. To the north of Port Appin is the irresistibly photogenic **Castle Stalker**. Standing on its own tiny island with a background of islands and hills, it's probably second only to the famous Eilean Donan in its portrayal of Scotland's romantic image. It was built upon the remnants of a previous MacDougall stronghold built in the 15th century by the Stewarts of Appin before falling into Campbell hands after the ill-fated 1745 rebellion. The current owners open it to the public for a limited period in July and August. Check opening times at the tourist office in Oban. **Castle Stalker View Café** overlooks the castle from the north and is a great place to eat and photograph the ancient site (see Restaurants, page 38).

Isle of Lismore → *Phone code 01631.*

The island of Lismore lies only a few miles off the mainland, in Loch Linnhe, yet feels a world away. It makes an ideal day trip and offers great opportunities for walking and cycling, as well as wonderful views across to the mountains of Morvern and Mull, the Paps of Jura to the south and Ben Nevis to the north. It's a fertile little island (the name *leis mór* is Gaelic for the big garden) that once supported a population of 1400, though the present population is only 176. Lismore has a long and interesting history as outlined by the award-winning, wood-clad **Gaelic Heritage Centre**, 'Ionad Naomh Moluag', which opened in 2007 complete with café and gift shop. Lismore was the ecclesiastical capital of Argyll for several centuries and the **Cathedral of St Moluag** was founded here in the 12th century, just north of Clachan. All that remains is the choir, which is now used as the parish church. The cathedral occupies the site of a church founded by the Irish saint, who established a religious community on the island about the same time as St Columba was busy at work in Iona. Legend has it that the two saints were racing to the island, in an attempt to be the first to land and found a monastery. Such was Moluag's religious zeal that he cut off his finger and threw it on to the shore, thus claiming possession. Not far from the church, is the 2000-year-old **Broch of Tirefour**, one of the best-preserved prehistoric monuments in Argyll, with surviving circular walls up to 16 ft high. Other sights include **Castle Coeffin**, a 13th-century fortress built by the MacDougalls of Lorn on the site of an earlier Viking settlement. In the southwest of the island lies the 13th-century **Achadun Castle**, built for the Bishops of Argyll. It's a short walk from here to **Bernera Island**, which can be reached at low tide (but don't get stranded).

South Lorn and the Slate Islands → *Phone code 01852.*

Eight miles south of Oban the B884 turns west off the A816 and wriggles its way round glassy lochs and knobbly, green hills studded with copper-coloured cattle to the tiny Slate Islands, so called because in the mid-19th century, the island's slate quarries exported millions of roofing slates every year. The quarrying industry has long since gone, leaving the area dotted with pretty little villages of whitewashed cottages.

The most northerly of the Slate Islands is **Seil** (or Clachan Seil), which is reached from the mainland across the seriously humpbacked Clachan Bridge. Better known as the 'Bridge over the Atlantic', it was built in 1792, with its high arch allowing ships to pass beneath. Beside the bridge is an old inn, **Tigh an Truish**, or 'House of the Trousers', where islanders once swapped their kilt for trousers in order to conform to the post-1745 ban on the wearing of Highland dress. There's also a petrol pump and souvenir shop here. Two miles south, at **Balvicar** (where there's a bank in the grocery store) the road turns right and climbs up and over to the harbour and attractive village of **Ellenabeich**, which is also, rather confusingly, known by the same name as the nearby island of Easdale. Ellenabeich is home to the Isle of Seil microbrewery (reputedly Scotland's smallest) since 2004. Before sinking a pint of their Corryveckan Ale, try the 130-yd, 12-hole Isle putting green. Apparently, if you beat the course par of 24, a bottle of Oban whisky is yours. The village is also the base for the excellent **Seafari Adventures** (see What to do, page 39), and here too you'll find the **Scottish Slate Islands Heritage Trust Centre** ① *T01852-300449, Apr-Oct daily 1030-1300, 1400-1700, £1.50, children 25p*, with its insight into the area's history.

Endearingly tiny **Easdale** is separated from Seil by a 500-yd-wide channel which has to be dredged to keep it open. The island, only 800 yds by 700 yds, was the centre of the slate industry and, between 1842 and 1861 produced over 130 million roof slates. Now inhabited by just 71 residents, the island once supported over 450 people before the quarries were flooded in the great storm of 1881 and the industry collapsed. A few minutes' walk from the ferry pier you'll find the delightful folk museum run by island volunteers. If the museum is closed, wander past the whitewashed former slate workers' cottages to seek out island information over a pint at the cosy **Puffer Bar**. The island's lively social life also revolves around the community hall with one of the highlights of the year being the keenly contested **World Stone-skimming Championships**, see Festivals, page 38. For more information on the island, visit www.easdale.org.

Another road runs south from Balvicar to **North Cuan**, from where the car ferry sails across the treacherous Cuan Sound to the long, thin island of **Luing** (pronounced 'Ling'). The island once had a population of around 600, which was drastically reduced during the Clearances to make way for cattle. Luing is still well known for its beef, and is the home of a successful new breed named after it. The island is small, 6 miles by 2 miles, and mostly flat, making it ideal for exploring by bike. Bikes can be hired just 50 yds from the ferry slipway at the **Sunnybrae Caravan Park** ① *T01852-314274*, from where static caravans can be hired from £100 per week. A mile or so further south is the village of **Cullipool**. The only other village is Toberonochy, 3 miles from Cullipool. Wildlife abounds with sightings of otters, seals, eagles and buzzards, whilst visitors can also enjoy a breathtaking panorama of the outlying isles of Mull, Shuna and Scarba.

South of the turn-off to the Slate Islands is **Arduaine Gardens** ① *T0844-493 2216, Apr-Sep daily 0930-1630, £5.50, concessions £4.40*, a beautiful place and an absolute must for all gardening enthusiasts. Gifted to the National Trust for Scotland in 1992, this 20-acre oasis boasts spectacular rhododendrons in early summer, Himalayan lilies, blue Tibetan poppies, a woodland garden, sweeping lawns and inspirational views across to Jura and the Slate Islands.

This is serious boating country, and just south of Arduaine, on the northern coast of the Craignish Peninsula, is surreal **Craobh Haven**, a yachting marina built in the style of a reproduction 18th-century fishing village. South of Craobh Haven is another yachting marina at **Ardfern**, where the **Galley of Lorne Hotel and pub** is invariably packed with yachties. You can arrange boat trips from Ardfern around Loch Craignish and to the offshore islands, see What to do, page 38.

Oban and around listings

For hotel and restaurant price codes and other relevant information, see pages 13-20.

● Where to stay

Oban *p31, map p32*

As the main ferry port for the islands, Oban gets busy in the summer with traffic. It's often an idea to get the tourist office to find you a bed; it'll cost more, but saves time and effort.

££££-£££ Manor House Hotel, Gallanach Rd, T01631-562087, www.manorhouse oban.com. Open year-round. 11 rooms. A beautiful stone house in a secluded location overlooking the bay on the road south towards the Kerrera ferry. Style and comfort assured and with a reputation for fine food.

£££ Caledonian Hotel, Station Sq, T0844-8559135, www.obancaledonian.com. Impressive former grand station built around 1882, overlooking the ferry pier. For a touch of luxury try one of the Captain's rooms with views across Oban bay. Coffee connoisseurs will enjoy the menu in the brasserie (**££**).

££ Alexandra Hotel, Corran Esplanade, T01631-562381. Large hotel with well-equipped rooms and good facilities, including pool and steam room.

££ Barriemore Hotel, Corran Esplanade, T01631-566356, www.barriemore-hotel.co.uk. Open Feb-Dec. A delightful, friendly guesthouse with great views of Oban Bay at the quieter end of the Esplanade. Very good value.

££ Dungallan House Hotel, Gallanach Rd, T01631-563799, www.dungallanhotel-oban.co.uk. Built in 1870 by the Duke of Argyll, this tastefully refurbished residence is another great Oban establishment that offers fine dining on locally sourced produce, over 100 malts and excellent views on the road south to the Kerrera ferry.

££ Glenburnie House, Corran Esplanade, T01631-562089, www.glenburnie.co.uk. Open Apr-Oct. A guesthouse renowned for tasteful rooms and excellent breakfasts, including fresh fruit salad and salmon with scrambled eggs.

££ Thornloe Guest House, Albert Rd, T01631-562879, www.thornloeoban.co.uk. Quiet and centrally located guesthouse offering 7 good-sized en suite rooms and limited off-street parking. Enjoy the sea views with a bottle of wine in the conservatory. One of the rooms has a 4-poster bed.

£ Jeremy Inglis Hostel, 21 Airds Cres, opposite the tourist office, T01631-565065. Handy for the train station and ferry, these small, quirky rooms include continental breakfast.

£ Oban Backpackers, Breadalbane St, T01631-562107, www.obanbackpackers.com. Open year-round and very popular. Book ahead.

£ SYHA Youth Hostel, Corran Esplanade, just beyond St Columba's Cathedral, T01631-562025. Open all year. With its 17 rooms and 6 dorms, this superbly equipped, friendly hostel is ideal for individuals and families who are looking for a safe, clean and hospitable budget option in Oban. Recommended.

Camping

Oban Caravan & Camping Park, Gallanach Rd, 2 miles south of town beyond the Kerrera ferry, T01631-562425. Open Apr to mid-Oct. Beautiful setting looking out to Kerrera but beware late-night revellers.

Roseview Caravan and Camping, on the Glenshellach Rd, 1.5 miles south of the ferry terminal, T01631-562755. Open Mar-Nov. Very good campsite with facilities for kids.

Around Oban *p33*

££££ Airds Hotel, Port Appin, T01631-730236, www.airds-hotel.com. One of Scotland's finest family-run hotels. The owners, Saun and Jenny McKivragan, ensure a personal touch pervades this classy establishment, which boasts exquisite views, fine dining and 11 delightful rooms. Recommended.

££££-£££ Willowburn Hotel, Seil, T01852-300276, www.willowburn.co.uk. Open Mar-Nov. 7 rooms with the rate including a delicious 4-course dinner. Just past the 'Bridge over the Atlantic' on Seil island, this house enjoys a delightful, peaceful setting with views over Sound of Seil. The owners bake their own bread, smoke their own salmon, duck and cheeses, and serve local produce including vegetables from the garden. An absolute gem. Recommended.

£££ Barcaldine Castle, Benderloch, 9 miles north of Oban and the A828, T01631-720598. Open year-round. This is a rare opportunity to reside in a 16th-century castle and home of the Campbells of Barcaldine (2 rooms available). You'll even step over the dungeon en route to breakfast.

£££ Loch Melfort Hotel, Arduaine, T01852-200233, www.lochmelfort.co.uk. Open all year. 23 rooms available. Terrific seafood and game as you enjoy the views over Asknish Bay.

£££ Pierhouse Hotel, Port Appin, T01631-730302, www.pierhousehotel.co.uk. Open all year. Looking out to the tiny pier and over Loch Linnhe, this stylish little hotel has a reputation for tasty, moderately priced local seafood. The 12 en suite rooms are tidy and comfortable. Also has a bar and pool room.

£ Kerrera Bunkhouse, Isle of Kerrera, T01631-570223, www.kerrerabunkhouse.co.uk. Open year-round. 6 rooms. Friendly accommodation complete with tea garden open May-Sep Wed-Sun 1030-1630.

Camping

Camping and Caravanning Club, Oban, Barcaldiine By Connel, Argyll, 12 miles north of Oban, T01631-720348. Open Apr-Oct. Clean and friendly.

Sunnybrae Caravan Park, South Cuan, Isle of Luing, T01852-314274. To enjoy fabulous sunsets towards Jura and an away-from-it-all escape, there's 1 of 6 static caravans for hire (£100-250 per week).

❼ Restaurants

Oban *p31, map p32*

£££ The Waterfront, 1 Railway Pier, T01631-563110. Daily 1000-1415, 1730-2130. Good seafood restaurant that owns 2 fishing boats, which land its daily catch. Pricey but the Waterfront Platter of langoustines, sea bass, scallops and garlic mussels is enticing.

£££-££ Coast, 104 George St, T01631-569900. Mon-Sat 1200-1400, 1730-2130, Sun 1730-2130. An imaginative menu in a stylish setting. Mouth-watering vegetarian, meat and seafood dishes served with a smile.

£££-££ The Studio Steakhouse, Craigard Rd, T01631-562030. Tue-Sun 1800-2100. A cosy restaurant away from the busy waterfront that serves a fine Stornoway black pudding starter and prime steaks in addition to its daily catch.

££ Ee'usk, North Pier, T01631-565666. Daily 1200-1500, 1800-2100. Busy, glass-fronted trendy fish restaurant, which isn't cheap but prides itself on the quality of its seafood. Service with flair. Huge seafood platter £59. Also good place for a rewarding lunch.

£ John Ogden's, by the ferry terminal. Daily 0900-1800. After 17 years, Ogden's bustling green shed remains Oban's best takeaway seafood haunt. For an inexpensive quality snack try a pot of squat lobster tails (£2.75), a fresh crab sandwich or the mouth-watering scallops in garlic (£6.75).

£ MacGillivray's Seafood Bar, just 20 m from **John Ogden's**. Offering the likes of pan fried scallops (£6) and squat lobster.

£ Nories, George St. After 43 years, it remains Oban's finest and friendliest chippy. Ask for it wrapped in newspaper.

Around Oban *p33*

£££ Airds Hotel, Port Appin, T01631-730236. Upmarket, award-winning fine dining that draws on the best of local seafood and Scottish meats. Recommended.

££££-££ Waypoint Bar and Grill, Isle of Kerrera, T01631-565333. From a hearty seafood platter to a humble BLT sandwich, hop aboard '*The Dirk*' at the North Pier in Oban to dine in style with lovely views across the bay. Ferry for guests only runs from 1210 daily.

££ The Oyster Inn, Connel Bridge, T01631-710666, www.oysterinn.co.uk. Modern, child-friendly restaurant with wide-ranging menu, real ales and sea views.

££-£ Castle Stalker View, Appin, T01631-730444. Feb-Oct daily 0930-1730, Nov-Dec Thu-Sun 1000-1600, Closed Jan. On the hillside overlooking the castle and directly off the Oban to Ballachulish main road, this is an excellent café. Tuck into the likes of Inverawe smoked salmon, freshly baked cakes and coffee. Panoramas down the sea lochs to Oban and unrivalled views over the castle. There are also information boards outlining the history of the castle and the infamous Appin murder. Outside, there's a path down to a viewpoint. Highly recommended.

££-£ Oyster Brewery and Restaurant, Ellenabeich Pier, Seil, T01852-300121. This harbourside hostelry is where to sample smooth real ales and a delicious seafood salad whilst bantering with the friendly locals.

🌙 Bars and clubs

Oban *p31, map p32*
Oban is no party town, but for an unrivalled taste of high energy and informal live ceilidh music head for **Skipinnish Ceilidh House** on George St, T01631-569599.
O'Donnells, Breadalbane St. Popular Irish bar.

Around Oban *p33*
You'll always find a pint and warm welcome at the **Galley of Lorne Hotel** in Ardfern; the **Puffer Bar** in Easdale; and the **Oyster Brewery Bar and Restaurant**, in Ellenabeich.

🎭 Entertainment

Oban *p31, map p32*
The Highland Theatre, at the north end of George St, T01631-562444. This is, confusingly, the local cinema. It shows most of the popular current releases.

🎉 Festivals

To check for major events in the area, visit www.eventscotland.org.

Oban *p31, map p32*
Apr-May Highlands & Islands Music & Dance Festival for Children, held at the end of Apr/beginning of May.
Aug Argyllshire Gathering (Oban Games), held during the 4th week of Aug in Mossfield Park, www.obangames.com.
Sep World Stone-skimming Championships, held on Easdale in late Sep, www.stone skimming.com. Drinking and merriment.

🏃 What to do

Oban *p31, map p32*
Boat trips
Boat trips can be made from Oban to Mull, Iona, Staffa and The Treshnish Islands with a variety of companies, including:
Argyll Charters, Corran Esplanade, T01631-563387; **Bowman's Tours**, Queens Park Pl, T01631-566809, in association with **Gordon Grant Tours** (Mull and Iona from Oban from £32); **Turus Mara**, Penmore Mill, Dervaig, Mull, T0800 0858786/01688-400242, www.turusmara.com.
Skipinnish Sea Tours, T07799-275388, T07714-764932, www.skipinnish-sea-tours.co.uk. For information and bookings contact the **Skipinnish Ceilidh House**, George St, T0161-569599. Open 1000-1800. Tickets can also be bought onboard. 1-hr trips around Kerrera cost £15, children £10. Tours run daily Apr-Oct and leave from the steps of Oban seafront.

Diving
Puffin Dive Centre, Gallanach Port, Gallanach Rd, T01631-566088, or booking office on George St, T01631-571190. This dive centre offers a 1½- to 2-hr beginner 'try-a-dive' (£87) and training for all standards including wreck diving.

Fishing
Oban Sea Fishing, Dunstaffnage Marina, T07793-120958, www.obanseafishing.com. Offshore fishing for all standards.

Swimming
Atlantis Leisure, Dalriach Rd, T01631-566800, www.atlantisleisure.co.uk. Sports and leisure centre with pool.

Around Oban *p33*
Boat trips
Craignish Cruises, T07747-023083, Ardfern Yacht Centre, T01852-500247, www.craignishcruises.co.uk. Runs private charters and fishing trips to the Sound of Jura, Corryvreckan and Garvellachs.
Seafari Adventures, Ellenabeich, Seil (also book at Oban TIC), T01852-300003, www.seafari.co.uk. Their 300 hp RIBS take you on a thrilling ride across the Corryvreckan whirlpool, with opportunities to spot seals, porpoises and lots of seabirds, £35, children £27. They also run a new Easdale to Iona day trip (departs 1030 and returns 1630) that's £70, under 16s £55. Travel to Iona to see the Abbey, ample time ashore, includes non landing trip to Staffa. Recommended.

Horse riding
Ardfern Riding Centre, Craobh Haven, T01852-500632. Offers a variety of trails and pub rides, from £23 for 1 hr.
Lettershuna Riding, Appin, T01631-730227. www.lettershunaridingcentre.com. Pony trekking.

Watersports
Linnhe Marine Watersports Centre, Lettershuna, just beyond Port Appin and 20 miles north of Oban, T07721-503981. Hire motor boats and sailing dinghies (from £35 for the 1st hr, £20 2nd hr and £10 thereafter).

⊘ Transport

Oban *p31, map p32*
Bus There are regular daily buses to **Inverness**, 4 hrs, via **Fort William** (1 hr 15 mins), **Benderloch** and **Appin** with Scottish Citylink, T08705-505050. Regular daily service to **Glasgow**, 3 hrs, with Scottish Citylink Coaches; Tue and Sat, 3 hrs with McGill's Bus, T01475-711122.

The **West Highland Flyer** minibus, T07780-724248, Easter-end Oct, links the **Oban** (Mull) and **Mallaig** (Skye) ferries. It will take you just 2½ hrs to do this route and the minibus will carry your bike. Departs Oban 0945 and arrives in Mallaig at 1215. Travels via Fort William and the Glen Nevis Youth Hostel on request.

Regular daily buses to **Dalmally**, via Cruachan Power Station, **Lochawe** and Taynuilt Hotel, with Awe Service Station, T01866-822612; Scottish Citylink, T08705-505050; and West Coast Motors, T01586-552319.

To **Ardrishaig**, via **Kilmartin** and **Lochgilphead**, Mon-Sat, **Scottish Citylink** and West Coast Motors, T01586-552319. To **Ellenabeich** and **North Cuan**, Mon-Sat, West Coast Motors.

Car hire Flit Van & Car Hire, Glencruitten Rd, T01631-566553. From £40 per day.

Cycle hire There are numerous cycling routes and walks in Argyll. Ask at the TIC for the leaflet, *Cycle the Forests of North Argyll*, or visit www.forestry.gov.uk/mtbscotland. Evo Bikes, 29 Lochside St, T01631-566996, rents bikes; Liberty Cycles, Unit 9, Mill Lane, T01631-564000. Rents adult, kids and trailer bikes from £15 per day.

Ferry Oban is the main ferry port for many of the Hebridean islands, for details of the CalMac ferry terminal, see page 31.

The departure point for ferries to **Kerrera** is 1.5 miles along the Gallanach Rd. They leave at regular intervals Mon-Fri 0845-1800, Sun 1030-1800.

A passenger ferry leaves to **Lismore island** Mon-Sat 4 times daily, twice on Sun, 50 mins, £5.80 return per passenger, £47.50 per car. A tiny passenger ferry sails from **Ellenabeich** on Seil to **Easdale**, making the 3-min trip at regular intervals Mon-Sat between 0745 and 2100, partly to schedule, partly on request. Ring the bell in the shelter on the pier (T01631-562125). A daily car ferry to **Luing** (South Cuan), T01631-562125, sails from South Cuan on Seil (5 mins), Mon-Sat every 15 mins from 0730 to 1820 (later in summer) and on Sun every 20 mins from 1100-1810. Return fare is £1.50 per passenger and £6.05 per car.

Train There are 3 trains daily to **Glasgow**, via **Crianlarich**, where the Oban train connects with the Mallaig/Fort William to Glasgow train.

Around Oban *p33*
Cycle hire **Isle of Luing Bike Hire**, Isle of Luing, T01852-314274. Hires bikes for £17 per day.

ⓘ Directory

Oban *p31, map p32*
Banks Several major banks have branches with ATMs in the centre of Oban and you can change foreign currency at the TIC. Note that some B&Bs and pubs on the islands will only take cash. **Internet** Oban SYHA; Oban Library, 77 Albany St, T01631-571444, free access.

Mid-Argyll, Kintyre, Cowal and Bute

Further south from Oban the long finger of Mid-Argyll extends past the offshore 'whisky isles' of Islay and Jura, pointing southwards into the remote Kintyre Peninsula where rolling hills protect the Isle of Arran from the wrath of the Atlantic Ocean. Packed with history, winding roads take visitors on a journey past attractive sea lochs and huge forests, revealing at Kilmartin Glen one of Europe's most important prehistoric sites. Mull of Kintyre is the lonely tip, a stone's throw from Northern Ireland. On the other side of Loch Fyne is the walking haven and giant claw of Cowal Peninsula, looking as if it's about to crush in its grasp the aptly named Isle of Bute, home to one of Scotland's most fantastical stately homes.

Tourist information

Cowal TIC ① *Alexandra Parade, Dunoon, T08707-200629, open all year*; **Helensburgh TIC** ① *clock tower on the waterfront, T01436-672642, open Apr-Oct*; **Bute TIC** ① *Promenade, Rothesay, T01700-502151, open all year*; **Inveraray TIC** ① *Front St, T01499-302063*; **Lochgoilphead TIC** ① *Lochnell St, T01546-602344, open Apr-Oct*; **Tarbert TIC** ① *Harbour St, T01880-820429*; and **Campbeltown TIC** ① *Old Quay, T01586-552056*.

Loch Awe and Loch Etive → *For listings, see pages 54-57.*

Loch Awe is the longest freshwater loch in Scotland and, further north, is the beautiful Loch Etive. Between the two Lochs runs the River Awe, which squeezes through the dark and ominous Pass of Brander. It is so steep and narrow that, according to legend, it was once held against the army by an old woman brandishing a scythe. There's enough to see here to justify a couple of days' exploration, particularly the little visited west shore of Loch Awe, and there are plenty of other places to visit around Inveraray to the south.

At the northeastern tip of Loch Awe, between the villages of of **Dalmally** and **Lochawe**, is the romantic ruin of **Kilchurn Castle**, on a promontory jutting out into the loch. It can be visited by boat from **Ardanaiseig Hotel** ① *T01866-833333*, on the east side of the loch. Also worth a look around here is the lovely, and rather bizarre, **St Conan's Church** ① *free, donation requested*, just off the A85 by Lochawe village. Built in the late 19th century but not used until 1930, the church's serene atmosphere is striking. Inside is an effigy of Robert the Bruce, with one of his bones buried underneath. The exterior, especially the south side overlooking the loch, is a riot of eccentric detail. You can buy fishing permits from the **Tight Line Bar** in the village.

Four miles west of Lochawe, and almost a mile inside Ben Cruachan (3695 ft) is the underground attraction of the **Cruachan Power Station or 'Hollow Mountain'** ① *Apr-Oct 0930-1645, Nov-Mar 1000-1700*. From the visitor centre on the shores of Loch Awe, a bus trip takes you into the heart of the mountain through tunnels until you reach the

Piscine cuisine

At **Inverawe Fisheries and Smokery**, see below, they buy smaller farmed salmon because they believe the lower fat content makes them tastier than larger ones. Traditional methods prevail here. The fish are dry salted, washed, smoked over oak logs for anything from 16 to 24 hours, depending on conditions, and then hand-sliced. The result is a rich and freshly oaky taste. From a 100 g smoked salmon pack (£7.50) to a 750 g pre-sliced side of salmon (£29.95), as well as gravadlax, smoked trout, eel and halibut, there's a diverse range to choose from.

Knipoch Smokehouse, South Lorn near Oban, T01852-316251, www.knipoch smokehouse.co.uk, on the other hand, believes that large salmon, 6-7 kg, produce the best quality. Its approach involves a dry salt cure strengthened with sugar, whisky, juniper and rowan berries, plus a lengthy two- to three-day smoke. The fish comes out so black it has to be washed and trimmed to look presentable, and the taste is rather unusual: strong, sweet, sharp and almondy. A whole side costs £45, but it can be cut to any size: sliced £17.60 per 500 g, unsliced £15.95. Also offer 500 g of smoked scallops for £22.

---

giant steel doors and generating room. Whilst exploring this Bond-like subterranean warren, it's impossible to forget the millions of tons of rock above your head. Pray Loch Awe doesn't spring a leak!

Further west, and 12 miles east of Oban, is the tiny village of **Taynuilt**, near the shore of Loch Etive. Just before the village, at Bridge of Awe, is a sign for **Inverawe Smokery and Fisheries** ① *T01866-822808, www.smokedsalmon.co.uk, Mar-Dec daily 0830-1700*, where you can take fishing lessons (£30), learn about traditional smoking techniques, or wander along a series of nature trails. If the weather's fine, you can buy some of their delicious smoked products and have a picnic, see box, above. If you fancy some smoked salmon delivered to your home, make sure you sign up for their mailing list.

One mile north of the village on the shores of Loch Etive is **Bonawe Iron Furnace** ① *T01866-822432, Apr-Sep daily 0930-1730, £4.50, concessions £3.60, children £2.70*. Founded in 1753 by a group of Cumbrian ironmasters, Bonawe used the abundant woodlands of Argyll to make charcoal to fire its massive furnace. At its height, it produced 600-700 tons of pig-iron a year and provided cannonballs for Admiral Nelson at the Battle of Trafalgar. Iron production ceased at Bonawe in 1876 and it has now been restored as an industrial heritage site, with displays explaining the whole production process.

Beyond Bonawe is the tranquil pier from which **Loch Etive Cruises** depart. Inaccessible except by boat, the cruise of one of Scotland's great hidden treasures is definitely worth it. ►► *See What to do, page 56.*

Running south from the village is the very lovely and very quiet Glen Lonan. Three miles along the Glen Lonan road is **Barguillean's Angus Garden** ① *T01866-822335, daily 0900-1800, £2*, one of Argyll's oldest and smallest gardens, but also one of the most peaceful and evocative, set around the shores of little Loch Angus. It was created in 1957, in memory of Angus MacDonald, a journalist and writer killed in Cyprus in 1956.

Walks around Loch Awe and Loch Etive

A single-track road runs southwest of Kilchrenan along the shores of Loch Awe to the tiny villages of **Dalavich** and **Ford**, through the very beautiful Inverinan Forest, a Forestry

Commission property which has a series of undemanding marked trails running through the hills overlooking the loch. The first walk starts out from the little hamlet of **Inverinan**. Red waymarkers lead you from the car park into the woods surrounding the gorge of the River Inan. Part of the route follows the old drove road along which cattle were driven from the Highlands down to the markets in south and central Scotland. The walk is 3 miles long and should take around 1½ hours. Further along the road, half a mile north of Dalavich, is a car park at **Barnaline Lodge**, the starting point for a 9-mile bike route, a way-marked walk through the Caledonian Forest Reserve, and a couple of other woodland walks. The longest of the walks is the 5-mile route that leads along the **River Avich**, then along the shores of **Loch Avich** before returning to the lodge. Two and a half miles south of Dalavich is a car park, which marks the starting point for a blue waymarked walk along the shores of **Loch Awe**. The route passes through **Mackenzie's Grove**, a sheltered gorge containing some of the largest conifers on the west coast. The route then runs along the shores of the loch, from where you can see the remains of a *crannog*, one of over 40 of these Iron Age settlements on Loch Awe. The route then heads back to the car park; about 3 miles in total. These routes are all outlined, with accompanying maps, in the Forestry Commission Scotland leaflet, *A Guide to Forest Walks and Trails in North Argyll*, available at tourist offices. Alternatively visit www.forestry.gov.uk/recreation.

Inveraray and around → *For listings, see pages 54-57.*

Inveraray → *Phone code 01499.*

Inveraray is the classic 18th-century planned town (don't call it a village), with its straight, wide streets and dignified Georgian houses, and enjoys the most stunning of settings, on the shores of Loch Fyne. It was rebuilt by the third Duke of Argyll, head of the Campbell clan, at the same time as he restored the nearby family home, which now attracts hordes of summer visitors. As well as its natural beauty and elegance, and fine castle, Inveraray has several other attractions that make an overnight stay in the town worthwhile. The sweet-toothed shouldn't walk past the door of **Sweet Memories** on Main Street East (open all year) where shelves are packed with jars of Scottish old world confectionery, including humbugs, aniseed balls and cough candy.

One of Argyll's most famous castles, **Inveraray Castle** ① *T01499-302203, Apr-Oct, Mon-Sun 1000-1745, (last admission 1700), £9, concessions £7.50, children £6.10, under 5s free*, has been the clan seat of the Campbells for centuries and is still the family home of the Duke of Argyll. The present neo-Gothic structure dates from 1745, and its main feature is the magnificent armoury hall, whose displays of weaponry were supplied to the Campbells by the British government to quell the Jacobite rebellion. The elaborately furnished rooms are also on display, as is the fascinating and troubled family history in the Clan room. For £1 from the TIC, the booklet *Five Walks on Inverary Estate* is a worthwhile investment.

Inveraray Jail ① *T01499-302381, Apr-Oct 0930-1800, Nov-Mar 1000-1700, £8.25, concessions £6.95, children £5.50*, the Georgian prison and courthouse in the centre of the town has been brilliantly restored as an interesting museum that gives a vivid insight into life behind bars from medieval times up until the 19th century. You can sit in on an 1820 courtroom trial, then visit the cells below and learn all about some of the delightful prison pursuits, such as branding with a hot iron, ear nailing and public whipping. The whole experience is further enhanced by the guides, who are dressed as warders and prisoners. Makes you want to stay on the right side of the law, although, thankfully, conditions have improved – as you will see for yourself.

Another worthwhile diversion, especially if you've got kids in tow, is the **Inveraray Maritime Museum** ① *T01499-302213, www.inveraraypier.com, daily 1000-1800, £5, concessions £3, children £2.50*, housed in the *SV Arctic Penguin*, one of the world's last iron sailing ships, which is moored at the lochside pier. Below deck are displays on Clyde shipbuilding, the Highland Clearances and footage from the maritime TV classic *Para Handy* as well as the chance to blow the foghorn and relax with an on-board cuppa. Berthed behind the ship is *Vital Spark*, an old Clyde 'puffer' which has been purchased by the museum. Your ticket to the Maritime Museum also entitles you to a 20% discount off the ticket price at the jail.

A few miles southwest of town, on the A83 to Lochgilphead, is **Argyll Adventure** ① *T01499-302611, www.argylladventure.com, Apr-Oct daily 1000-1700, from £6 per activity*. Here, by the banks of Loch Fyne, both children and the young at heart can indulge in laser clay-pigeon shooting, Laser Quest, bungee trampolining, climbing and horse riding (from £25). Call ahead to book pony treks/riding.

Three miles beyond Argyll Adventure is **Auchindrain Township** ① *T01499-500235, www.auchindrain-museum.org.uk, Apr-Oct daily 1000-1700 (last admission 1600), £5.50, concessions £4.50, children £3*, a restored and authentic West Highland farming village with parts dating to the 1700s. Features include two perfectly restored thatched cottages and barns, furnished and equipped with dairy and household items to give a real insight into what rural life must have been like in centuries past. There's also an informative visitor centre and coffee shop. Recommended.

Four miles further down the A83 is **Crarae Gardens** ① *T01546-886614, visitor centre Apr-Oct daily 1000-1700, gardens open all year daily 0930-sunset, £6, concessions £5*, one of Scotland's very best public gardens, dramatically set in a deep wooded glen on the shores of Loch Fyne. Initiated by Lady Campbell in 1912, there are marked woodland walks winding their way through a spectacular array of rhododendrons, azaleas and numerous other exotic plants towards the tumbling waterfalls of the 'Himalayan Gorge'. Any time of year is rewarding to visit including autumn when foliage is resplendent in rich tints.

Kilmartin and around → *Phone code 01546.*

Much of this region was once part of the ancient Kingdom of Dalriada, established by the Irish Celts (known as the *Scotti*, hence Scotland) who settled here in the fifth century. North of Lochgilphead, on the A816 to Oban, is **Kilmartin Glen**, an area of Neolithic and Bronze Age chambered and round cairns, stone circles, rock carvings, Iron Age forts and duns, Early Christian sculptured stones and medieval castles. Indeed, there are more than 350 ancient monuments within just a few miles radius of **Kilmartin House Museum** ① *T01546-510278, Mar-Oct 1000-1730, Nov-Dec 1100-1600, £4.60, concessions £3.90, children £1.70*. Housed in the old manse next to the parish church in the tiny village of **Kilmartin**, the 15-minute audio-visual display and imaginative exhibits provide an invaluable insight into the surrounding landscape. The **Glebe Cairn Café** is well worth a visit. Next door in the church graveyard are the Kilmartin crosses, dating from as far back as the ninth and 10th centuries. Also within the graveyard is one of the largest collections of medieval grave slabs in the West Highlands.

Two miles north of Kilmartin, sitting high above the A816, is **Carnasserie Castle** ① *free, it's a little way from the car park*, an imposing 16th-century tower house built by John Carswell, Bishop of the Isles, who translated *The Book of the Common Order* in 1567, the first book to be printed in Gaelic.

Most notable of all is the **linear cemetery**, a line of burial cairns that stretch southward from Kilmartin village for over 2 miles. The largest and oldest of the group is the Neolithic cairn, Nether Largie South, which is over 5000 years old and big enough to enter. The other cairns, Nether Largie North, Mid Nether Largie and Ri Cruin, are Bronze Age, and the huge stone coffins show carvings on the grave slabs. Nearby are the Temple Wood Stone Circles, where burials took place from Neolithic times to the Bronze Age.

On the other side of the A816, and visible from the road, is a group of monuments which can all be reached from Dunchraigaig Cairn. This is a huge Bronze Age cairn with some of the covering stones removed to reveal three stone coffins. From here a path is signed to **Ballymeanoch Standing Stones**, the tallest of which is 12-ft high. Two of the stones are decorated with cup marks, prehistoric rock carvings that can be found at numerous locations throughout the Kilmartin area. There's also a henge monument in the same field. These were generally round or oval platforms with an internal ditch, and it's thought they were used for ceremonial purposes. The best example of rock carvings is at Achnabreck, near Cairnbaan village, the largest collection anywhere in Britain. The purpose and significance of these cup- and ring-marked rocks is still a matter of debate.

A few miles south of Kilmartin village is the Iron Age hill fort of **Dunadd**, which stands atop a rocky outcrop and dominates the surrounding flat expanse of **Moine Mhór** (Great Moss), one of the few remaining peat bogs in the country and now a nature reserve. **Dunadd Fort** became the capital of the ancient kingdom of Dalriada around AD 500 and is one of the most important Celtic sites in Scotland. The views from the top are wonderful and worth the visit alone, but you can also see carved out of the exposed rock, a basin and footprint, thought to have been used in the inauguration ceremonies of the ancient kings of Dalriada.

Crinan Canal

Kilmartin Glen is bordered to the south by the Crinan Canal, a 9-mile stretch of waterway linking Loch Fyne at Ardrishaig with the Sound of Jura. It was designed and built by Sir John Rennie in 1801, with the assistance of the ubiquitous Thomas Telford, to allow shipping to avoid the long and often hazardous journey round the Mull of Kintyre and to help stimulate trade in the islands. These days you're more likely to see pleasure yachts and cruisers sailing on the canal than the cargo vessels, which once transported coal and other goods to the islands and returned with livestock. You don't need to come in a boat to appreciate the canal. You can walk or cycle along the towpath that runs the entire length of the canal, from Ardrishaig to Crinan, and watch boats of all shapes and sizes negotiating a total of 15 locks. The best place to view the canal traffic is at **Crinan**, a pretty little fishing port on Loch Crinan at the western end of the canal.

Knapdale

Running south from the Crinan Canal down to Kintyre is Knapdale, a forested, hilly area that gets its name from its Gaelic description, *cnap* (hill) and *dall* (field). It's an area worth exploring, for there are many walking and cycling trails and superb views from the west coast across to the Paps of Jura. Immediately south of the canal is Knapdale Forest, which stretches from coast to coast over hills dotted with tiny lochs. Forestry Commission Scotland has marked out several trails. Three fairly easy circular routes start from the B8025 which runs south from **Bellanoch**, just east of Crinan.

One trail sets out from the car park at the unmanned Barnluasgan Interpretation Centre and runs up to a point beyond **Loch Barnluasgan**, with great views over the forest and the many lochs. It's a mile in total. A second trail, also a mile long, starts from a car park a little further along the B8025 and heads through the forest to the deserted township of **Arichonan**. The third trail starts out from the car park between the starting points for the first and second trails. It runs right around **Loch Coille-Bharr** and is 3 miles long. A more strenuous walk starts from a car park about 100 yds into the forest, off the B841, about half a mile west of Cairnbaan, and climbs up to the peak of **Dunardy** (702 ft).

At the Barnluasgan Interpretation Centre a little side road turns south down the eastern shore of beautiful Loch Sween, past the village of Achnamara, to the 12th-century **Castle Sween**. First impressions of the castle, situated on the shores of the lovely loch with the forested hills all around, are tainted by the sprawling caravan park and self-catering chalets on a nearby 15,000-acre estate. Unfortunately, the caravans were not there when Robert the Bruce attacked the castle, otherwise he might have done us all a favour by razing them. Three miles south is the ruined 13th-century **Kilmory Knap Chapel**. A new glass roof protects the carved stones inside. Here, visitors will find an 8-ft-high, 15th-century **MacMillan's Cross**, which shows the Crucifixion on one side and a hunting scene on the other. There are also several unmarked graves, believed to be those of 13th-century Knights Templar who fled from France.

Lochgilphead

The main town in the area of Mid-Argyll, and administrative centre for the entire Argyll and Bute region, is Lochgilphead, a sleepy little place at the head of Loch Gilp, an arm of Loch Fyne. Lochgilphead started life as a planned town, but the industries came and went, leaving it with the customary grid plan of wide streets but little else. Today it serves as a useful base for exploring the area, with accommodation options, a bank and a supermarket. There's a nice easy walk from the car park at Kilmory Castle Gardens, about a mile east of town, up to Kilmory Loch. It takes about an hour there and back and is well marked. The gardens also make a pleasant stroll and there are other marked walks, including up to **Dun Mór** (360 ft).

Kintyre → *For listings, see pages 54-57. Phone code 01880.*

The long peninsula of Kintyre is probably best known as the inspiration for Paul McCartney's phenomenally successful 1970s dirge, *Mull of Kintyre*, but don't let that put you off. Historic Kintyre may be isolated but it's also packed with great scenery, wildlife and beaches, which attract the experienced surfer and windsurfer alike. Hardy walkers also have the opportunity to explore the 89-mile **Kintyre Way coastal route** ① *www. kintyreway.com*, stretching from Tarbert harbour to Dunaverty in the south. The peninsula would be an island, were it not for the mile-long isthmus between West and East Loch Tarbert, a fact not lost on King Magnus Barefoot of Norway. In the 11th century he signed a treaty with the Scottish king, Malcolm Canmore, giving him all the land he could sail round, and promptly had his men drag his longboat across the narrow isthmus, thus adding Kintyre to his kingdom.

Arriving in Kintyre

Getting there There is at least one flight daily (35 minutes) from Glasgow to Campbeltown (Machrihanish) airport. For times and reservations, contact **Flybe** ① *www.flybe.com T0871-700 2000*. There are several daily **Citylink buses** ① *T0844-266 3333*, from Glasgow to Campbeltown (4½ hours) via Inveraray, Lochgilphead, Kennacraig and Tarbert.

Getting around Public transport on Kintyre has improved, though still requires patience. On the west coast there's a regular (daily) bus service running between Campbeltown,

Tarbert, Lochgilphead and Glasgow that also stops at the Kennacraig ferry terminal (for crossings to Islay). From Tarbert to Claonaig (for ferries to Lochranza on Arran) and Skipness there are buses Monday to Saturday. A bus also covers the quiet east route between Campbeltown and Carradale. Details are available from **Argyll & Bute Council** ① *T01546-602127*, or **Tarbert TIC** ① *Main St, T08707-200023, open Apr-Oct.* ▸▸ *See Transport, page 57.*

Tarbert

The fishing village of Tarbert sits at the head of East Loch Tarbert, in a sheltered bay backed by forested hills, and is one the most attractive ports on the west coast. Tarbert (the name derives from the Gaelic *An Tairbeart*, meaning 'isthmus') has a long tradition of fishing, and in the 18th and 19th centuries was a major herring port. Today, prawns and other shellfish are the main catch and though there is still a sizeable fleet, fishing has declined in importance to the local economy. Tourism is now a major source of income, with yachties in particular swelling local coffers when the **Scottish Series**, the second largest yacht race in the UK sails into the picturesque natural harbour.

Overlooking the harbour is the dramatically sited ruin of **Robert the Bruce's 14th-century castle**. There's not much left to see, other than the five-storey 15th-century keep. It's unsafe to investigate the ruins too closely, but the view alone is worth the walk. There are steps leading up to the castle, next to the **Loch Fyne Gallery** on Harbour Street. Behind the castle there are several marked trails leading up into the hills, with great views over Loch Fyne and the islands. Less strenuous is the short walk at the end of Garvel Road, on the north side of the harbour, which leads to the beach. At the end of East Pier road, beyond the Cowal Ferry, is yet another good walk, to the **Shell Beaches**. One mile south, you can also explore the lovely gardens at **Stonefield Castle Hotel**, see Where to stay, page 54.

Gigha → *www.isle-of-gigha.co.uk.*

The small island of Gigha (pronounced *Gee-a* with a hard 'g') translates from Norse as 'God's Island'. A grand claim, perhaps, but there's no question that this most accessible of islands is also one of the loveliest (and pretty much midge-free). It's only a 20-minute ferry ride away, and is only 7 miles by 1 mile, so it can be visited easily in a day, which is just about enough time to appreciate why the Vikings loved it so much. Like so many of the Hebridean islands, Gigha has had a long list of owners, including various branches of the MacNeils and, more recently, in 1944, Sir James Horlick, he of bedtime drink fame. Now, though, the islanders are the proud owners of their own little piece of paradise, thanks to a successful buy-out in 2001.

It was Horlick who created the islanders self-proclaimed 'Jewel in the Crown'; the wonderful **Achamore Gardens** ① *1 mile south of the ferry terminal, T01583-505254, daily 0900-dusk, £2.* Thanks to Gigha's mild climate, the 50-acre woodland garden has an amazing variety of tropical plants, including rhododendrons, azaleas and camellias. The sight of albino peacocks and palm trees may have you doubting this is a Scottish island at all. There are two marked walks, starting from the walled garden. Managed by the Isle of Gigha Heritage Trust, a three-year, £600,000 garden restoration project has ensured Gigha's 'jewel' continues to shine for years to come.

The island's other delights include some good walks, white sandy beaches and fantastic views across to Jura on one side and Kintyre on the other. One of the best walks is to take the path left after the nine-hole golf course, signed Ardaily, past Mill Loch to the **Mill** on the west shore. The views from here are just magnificent. Another good idea is to walk, or cycle to the peninsula of **Eilean Garbh** at the north of the island. About half a mile beyond

Kinererach Farm a path leads left to the peninsula where two crescent-shaped beaches are separated by a thin spit of land. And if the weather's good enough for a picnic, make sure you try some of the island's famously distinctive cheese.

Campbeltown and around

At the southern end of the Kintyre Peninsula is **Campbeltown**, once home to 34 whisky distilleries and a large fishing fleet. Still the largest town in Kintyre, the two remaining distilleries hint at the town's decline in fortune, though the **Campbeltown Heritage Centre** ① *T07733-485387, Apr-Sep Mon-Sat 1130-1630, £2*, richly documents its history. Another worthwhile local attraction is the **Scottish Owl Centre** ① *Witchburn Rd, T01586-554397, Apr, May, Jun and Sep Wed-Sat, Jul-Aug Mon-Sat 1330-1630, with flying display at 1430, £6, children £4*. Six miles west lies **Machrihanish** and until recently a secretive military airbase beyond which miles of golden sands and gigantic Atlantic breakers beckon beachcombers and experienced wave-sailors alike. Nearby is a dramatic 18-hole championship golf course. The beach can be approached either by walking north from the village, or south from the car park on the main A83 to Tayinloan and Tarbert, where it leaves the coast.

If the weather's good, it's worth taking a walk up to **Beinn Ghulean**, which overlooks the town and loch. Follow the signs for the A83 to Machrihanish until you reach Witchburn Road. After passing the creamery on your left, turn left into Tomaig Road and continue until you come to a wooden gate. Cross over the stile and follow the track through the fields, crossing two more stiles, before you reach the Forest Enterprise sign which marks the start of the walk. It's about 4 miles there and back from the end of Tomaig Road.

One of the most popular day trips is to the uninhabited **Davaar Island**, connected to the peninsula by a tidal breakwater. Here you can see the cave painting of the Crucifixion, completed in secret by a local artist in 1877. The island can be visited at low tide from Kildalloig Point, a couple of miles east of town. Check tide times at the tourist office before setting out.

It's only a short drive south from Campbeltown to the tip of the peninsula, the Mull of Kintyre. There's nothing much to see in this bleak, storm-battered place, apart from the coast of Ireland, a mere 12 miles away and clearly visible on a good day. The road out to the lighthouse, built in 1788 and remodelled by Robert Stevenson, grandfather of Robert Louis, is both twisty and spectacular. Above the lighthouse is a small poignant cairn in memory to military personnel killed when their helicopter crashed in bad weather about a decade ago on the remote hillside. It's possible to walk from here up to Machrihanish (about 10 miles), past the ruined township of **Balmavicar** and the **Largiebaan Bird Reserve**. The views are great and there's a chance of seeing golden eagles.

The southernmost village on Kintyre is **Southend**, a bleak, windswept place with a wide sandy beach. At the east end of the beach, jutting out on a rocky promontory, are the scant remains of **Dunaverty Castle**, once a MacDonald stronghold, where 300 Royalists were brutally massacred in 1647 by the Covenanting army of the Earl of Argyll, despite having already surrendered. To the west of Southend, below the cliffs, is the ruined 13th-century **Keil Chapel**, which is said to mark the spot where St Columba first set foot on Scottish soil, before heading north to Iona. Close by is a pair of footprints carved into the rock, known as Columba's footprints.

The slow and winding single track B842 meanders up the east coast from Campbeltown to Skipness and Claonaig, departure point for the ferry to Arran, see page 58. The scenery en route is gentle and pleasant, with nice views of Arran, and there are some worthwhile places to stop.

Ten miles up the coast are the idyllic ruins of **Saddell Abbey**, a Cistercian establishment founded by Somerled in 1160. The abbey fell into ruin in the early 16th century and much of the stone was used in the building of 18th-century Saddell Castle for the Bishop of Argyll. Though little remains, there are some impressive medieval grave slabs, depicting knights, monks, ships, animals and other images.

A few miles further north is the village of **Carradale**, the only place of any size on the east coast, nestling in the sandy sweep of beautiful Carradale Bay. There are several pleasant marked walks through the woods between the B842 and the shore. The shortest of these walks (with green waymarkers) starts from the Network Centre (see below) and is a mile long. There's a 3-mile walk with red waymarkers which starts at the **Port Na Storm** car park and follows the forest road to the left. After 150 yds the route turns left again at the road junction. A mile further on, you turn right off the road and follow the track up to the summit of **Cnoc-nan Gabhor**, from where there are great views of Kintyre and across to Arran. A third walk (6 miles; blue waymarkers) also starts from the Port Na Storm car park. This time the route heads right at the junction 150 yds beyond the car park and then runs north along the shore, with a chance of seeing dolphins and basking shark. The path then swings west towards the road, then turns south with views of Carradale Glen.

Twelve miles north of Carradale the B842 ends at **Claonaig**, which is actually nothing more than a slipway for the ferry to Arran (see page 58). From here the B8001 heads west to meet the A83 near the Kennacraig ferry pier. A dead-end road runs north for a few miles to the tiny village of **Skipness**, where you can visit the substantial ruins of the 13th-century Skipness Castle and nearby chapel.

Cowal Peninsula and the Clyde Coast → *For listings, see pages 54-57.*

The Cowal Peninsula reaches out into the Firth of Clyde, framed by Loch Fyne and Loch Long. This is the most visited part of Argyll due to its proximity to Glasgow, but, despite the summer hordes, many of whom come for the Cowal Highland Gathering in late August, much of it is undisturbed. Most people head straight for the rather drab main ferry port and traditional Clyde seaside resort of Dunoon. More adventurous souls enjoy the forests and mountains of Argyll Forest Park in the north or the peace of the southwest coastline.

Argyll Forest Park
The northern part of the peninsula is largely covered by the sprawling Argyll Forest Park which extends from Loch Lomond south to Holy Loch. This area contains the most stunning scenery in Cowal, and includes the **Arrochar Alps**, a range of rugged peaks north of Glen Croe which offer some of the best climbing in Argyll. The most famous of these is anvil-like Ben Arthur (2891 ft), better known as **The Cobbler**. Less imposing are the hills south of Glen Croe, between Loch Goil and Loch Long, in an area known as Argyll's Bowling Green (not because it's flat, but an English corruption of the Gaelic *Baile na Greine*, meaning 'Sunny Hamlet'). There are many footpaths and cycle tracks threading their way through the park. Details of five are outlined in the excellent *Argyll Forest Park Guide* (£3), available from the Forestry Commission office in Ardgarten.

Arrochar to Dunoon
The gateway to Cowal, Arrochar sits at the head of Loch Long on the main A83, only a few miles west of Tarbet and the shores of Loch Lomond. It's a small, uninspiring place but the setting is dramatic, with The Cobbler towering overhead. A few miles beyond Arrochar, on

the shores of Loch Long, is **Ardgarten**, where there's an excellent **Forestry Commission Visitor Centre** ⓘ *T01301-702436, Apr-Oct daily 1000-1700*. This provides useful information on hillwalking and wildlife and is an excellent start-point for climbing The Cobbler (seven hours return trip). From Ardgarten, the A83 climbs steeply up Glen Croe to reach one of Scotland's classic viewpoints at the top of the pass, the **Rest and be Thankful** (built under Major Caulfeild after the '45). The hordes of like-minded tourists, eager for that memorable photograph, cannot detract from the majestic views of the surrounding craggy peaks.

Here the road forks. The A83 continues towards **Inveraray**, see page 43, and the single-track B828 heads southwest to meet the B839, which runs down to the village of **Lochgoilhead**, in a beautiful setting on Loch Goil. There are several hotels and B&Bs as well as an unsightly village of self-catering holiday chalets next door. At the end of the road, several miles down the west side of Loch Goil, are the ruins of 15th-century **Carrick Castle**.

The A83 meanwhile runs down through **Glen Kinglas** to reach the village of **Cairndow**, at the head of Loch Fyne. Here, gastronomes must decide whether to drive south down the A815 and east side of Loch Fyne for Inver Cottage, by Castle Lachlan, or continue towards Inveraray and **Clachan**, to dine in the ever popular **Loch Fyne Oyster Bar**, see page 55. At the southern end of Loch Eck, at Benmore, is the **Younger Botanic Garden** ⓘ *T01369-706261, Apr-Sep daily 1000-1800, Mar and Oct 1000-1700, £5, concessions £4, children £1*, a lovely woodland garden and offshoot of the Royal Botanic Garden in Edinburgh. Its 120 acres are laid out with over 300 species of rhododendrons and feature an avenue of giant redwoods.

Dunoon

The largest town in Cowal, with around 8000 inhabitants, is Dunoon, one-time favourite holiday destination for Glaswegians, who came in their hordes on board the many paddle steamers that sailed "doon the watter" from Glasgow. Dunoon still attracts many visitors, but the town's economy has suffered following the closure of the Holy Loch US nuclear submarine in the 1990s. Nevertheless, Dunoon still comes to life during the **Cowal Highland Gathering**, see page 56. There's not much to detain you here, although the **Castle House Museum** ⓘ *Easter-Oct Mon-Sat 1030-1630, Sun 1400-1630, £2, concessions £1.50, children free*, on Castle Hill overlooking the town offers an insight into clan history and the role of the Clyde in wartime, and allows you to bone up on Cowal's often grisly past. There are **CalMac** ferries every hour (0620-2020) from Gourock to Dunoon, with train connections from Glasgow Central (25 minutes, £3.20 one way per person, £8.80 per car). There is also a ferry service from McInroy's Point, 2 miles from Gourock, with **Western Ferries** ⓘ *www.western-ferries.co.uk*. It leaves every 15-20 minutes during peak times and runs daily from 0730-2400, £3.50 per passenger, £9.90 per car.

The southwest

One of the most beautiful parts of Argyll is the southwest of Cowal, particularly the route down to the little village of **Tighnabruaich**. The A8003 runs down the west side of Loch Riddon and there are few lovelier sights than the view from this road across the **Kyles of Bute**, the narrow straits that separate Cowal from the island of Bute. Tighnabruaich gets busy in the summer with visitors who come here to enjoy the best sailing on the west coast. A few miles southwest of Kames is **Portavadie**, on the west coast of Cowal. A **CalMac** car and passenger ferry sails from here to Tarbert, on the Kintyre Peninsula, saving a lot of time if you're heading for the islands of Islay, Jura or Colonsay.

Helensburgh

Overlooking the Clyde is the town of Helensburgh, its wide, grid-plan streets lined with elegant Georgian houses. The town is most famously known for its connection with the great Glasgow architect, **Charles Rennie Mackintosh**. In the upper part of the town is **Hill House** ① *Upper Colquhoun St, T01436-673900, Apr-Oct daily 1330-1730, £9, concessions £6.50, tea room open 1330-1630, trains from Glasgow Queen Street station to Helensburgh Central*, one of the best examples of Mackintosh's work. The house was designed for Glasgow publisher Walter Blackie in 1902-1904, and is managed by the National Trust for Scotland. In accordance with Blackie's wish to have a house with an individual feel, it is a masterpiece of balanced perfection and artistry with great attention to detail. The use of light and dark, and the symbolism of the floral patterns – hallmarks of his personal art nouveau style – are in evidence. After exploring the house, visit the cosy tea room in the converted kitchen.

Isle of Bute → *For listings, see pages 54-57.*

Barely a stone's throw off the south coast of Cowal is the island of Bute, another favourite holiday destination for people from Glasgow and Ayrshire, who come here in droves during the busy summer months. But though the island is small (15 miles long by 5 miles wide), it's deceptively easy to escape the hordes, who tend to congregate around the east coast resort of Rothesay, leaving the delights of the sparsely populated west coast free for those who enjoy a bit of peace and quiet.

Bute

Arriving on the Isle of Bute

Getting there The bus service provided by West Coast Motors is good, though limited on Sunday. There are buses to Rothesay from Tighnabruaich in southwest Cowal at least once a day from April to October, the journey takes one hour. For times, contact **West Coast Motors** ① *T0870-850 6687*. A car/passenger ferry makes the five-minute crossing from Colintraive to Rhubodach, at the northern end of Bute, daily every 30 minutes or hour from Easter until the end of August (Monday-Saturday 0530-2055 and Sunday 0830-2055). It costs £1.40 one way per person and £8.80 per car. Bute is easily accessible from Glasgow. Take a train from Glasgow Central to the ferry terminal at Wemyss Bay, and from there it's a 35-minute crossing to Rothesay. The ferries leave every 45 minutes from 0715 until 1945 (later on Friday, Saturday and Sunday), £4.45 one way per passenger, £17.60 per car. For times and fares, call T08705-650000.

Getting around The best way to see Bute is still by bike, with roads fairly quiet and in good condition beyond Rothesay. The No 93 bus makes at least five trips daily between Guildford Square in Rothesay and Mount Stuart.

Rothesay

The sole town on Bute is Rothesay, with its handsome period mansions lining the broad sweep of bay, its elegant promenade lined with palm trees and the distinctive 1920s **Winter Gardens**, now refurbished with a cinema, restaurant and the TIC. **Rothesay Castle** ① *T01700-502691, Mon-Sat 0930-1900, closed Thu and Fri afternoon in winter, £4.50, concessions £3.60, children £2.70.* One thing men must do before leaving Rothesay is visit the palatial **Victorian public toilets** ① *Easter-Sep daily 0800-2100, Oct-Mar daily 0900-1700.* This architectural gem enables gents to 'spend a penny' in style.

Mount Stuart

① *T01700-503877, www.mountstuart.com. House and grounds open May-Sep daily 1200-1700, grounds 1000-1800. House and grounds £8, concessions £6.50, children £4; grounds only £4, concessions £3.50, children £2.50.*

One of Bute's main attractions is Mount Stuart, a unique Victorian Gothic house set in 300 acres of lush woodland gardens, 3 miles south of Rothesay. This magnificent architectural fantasy reflects the Third Marquess of Bute's passion for astrology, astronomy, mysticism and religion, and the sheer scale and grandeur of the place almost beggars belief. This is truly one of the great country houses of Scotland and displays breathtaking craftsmanship in marble and stained glass, as well as a fine collection of family portraits and Italian antiques. Much of the existing house dates from 1877, and was built following a terrible fire which destroyed the original, built in 1719 by the Second Earl of Bute. Equally impressive are the landscaped gardens and woodlands, established by the Third Earl of Bute (1713-1792), who advised on the foundation of Kew Gardens in London, and the stunning visitor centre complete with audio-visuals and restaurant. The present owner is Johnny Dumfries (only the Daily Mail calls him the Seventh Marquess of Bute), former racing driver who won Le Mans in 1988 and who, famously, gave up his house for the wedding of Stella McCartney, daughter of Paul, in 2003. It's worth spending a whole day here in order to take in the splendour of the house and to explore the beautiful gardens. And if the weather's fine, why not bring a picnic and enjoy the wonderful sea views.

Other places around the island

Just before Mount Stuart is the tidy little village of **Kerrycroy**, designed by the wife of the Second Marquess of Bute and featuring an interesting mix of building styles. South of Mount Stuart and the village of Kingarth is **Kilchattan Bay**, an attractive bay of pink sands and the start of a fine walk down to Glencallum Bay, in the southeastern corner of the island.

Southwest of Kilchattan Bay is **St Blane's Chapel**, a 12th-century ruin in a beautifully peaceful spot near the southern tip of the island. The medieval church stands on the site of an earlier monastery, established in the sixth century by St Blane, nephew of St Catan, after whom Kilchattan is named. The ruin can be reached by road from Rothesay, or as part of the walk from Kilchattan Bay. Four miles north of St Blane's, on the west coast, is **Scalpsie Bay**, the nicest beach on the island and a good place for seal spotting. A little further north is **St Ninian's Point**, looking across to the island of **Inchmarnock**. At the end of the beach are the ruins of a sixth-century chapel, dedicated to St Ninian.

The Highland–Lowland dividing line passes through the middle of Bute at Loch Fad, which separates the hilly and uninhabited northern half of the island and the rolling farmland of the south. The highest point on the island is **Windy Hill** (913 ft) in the north, from where there are great views across the island. A less strenuous walk is up **Canada Hill**, a few miles southwest of Rothesay, above Loch Fad. Walk along Craigmore promenade and turn off at the old pier to **Ardencraig Gardens**. Then continue uphill along the golf course to the top of the hill for great views of the Firth of Clyde.

Kilchattan Bay to Glencallum Bay walk

A longer walk is the circular route from Kilchattan Bay south to Glencallum Bay and back, via St Blane's chapel. The bay was once a final staging point for boats bound for overseas. The walk is 5 miles in total. Allow about four hours. There are buses to and from Rothesay. The route is waymarked, but if you want to take a map, it's OS Landranger sheet 63 or Explorer 362. The Rothesay Discovery Centre (TIC) carries a full stock of maps.

Follow the signpost for 'Kelspoke Path' beside Kiln Villas and take the track, which climbs steadily before turning sharply back on itself. Go through a gate and shortly before the next gate turn right. Follow the rough track, which swings right, then left over open ground to the ruins of Kelspoke Castle.

Continue along the grassy path, past a reservoir on your right, then cross the stile and go down and across a small burn. Turn left and follow the burn, before heading right to join the shore path and follow this past the lighthouse on your left and around the headland to **Glencallum Bay**. Continue round the shoreline and at the far end of the bay follow the waymarks as the path climbs to cross the headland. The path then levels out and from here there are great views across to the mountains of Arran.

The path then reaches the col above **Loch na Leighe**. Drop down to the loch and follow the waymarks south over open ground. Before reaching a farm called The Plan, go right over two footbridges, then left below a low ridge. Keep to the right of the buildings, following the waymarks across open ground to the stile that crosses to the ruins of St Blane's Chapel (see above). Leave the chapel by the gap in the boundary wall and go through a gate, turning left on a clear track which climbs steadily to a stile. Cross the stile and turn right, following the edge of the field down to a gate. Walk uphill on the left side of the field to Suidhe Hill. At the top of the field, cross the fence and keep going, turning right at the corner of the fence. Go through a gate at the next corner and look for a waymark about 100 yds downhill. Follow the path steeply downhill, passing through a kissing gate and staying close to the wall. You then reach a drying green at the foot of the hill; turn left and follow a path around the buildings and back onto the road at **Kilchattan**.

Mid-Argyll, Kintyre, Cowal and Bute listings

For hotel and restaurant price codes and other relevant information, see pages 13-20.

⬤ Where to stay

Loch Awe and Loch Etive *p41*
££££ Ardanaiseig Hotel, 3 miles east of Kilchrenan village (12 miles from Taynuilt) on an unclassified road, T01866-833333, www.ardanaiseig-hotel.com. Open Feb-Dec. A luxurious highland retreat that boasts one of the best hotel restaurants in Scotland (**£££**). You'll pay at least £50 per head for dinner but with delicious food, a delightful ambience (including drinks by the fire in the library bar) and even private boat trips to atmospheric Kilchurn Castle, it's 1st class.
££ Blarcreen Farm, Ardchattan Estate, T01631-750272, www.blarcreenfarm.com. Open Mar-Dec. A mile past Ardchattan Priory on the road from Oban to Bonawe. Elegant, Victorian farmhouse standing on its own surrounded by lovely countryside. Individually styled rooms, homely ambience and 3-course candlelit dinner from £28.50 per person.

Self-catering
Inistrynich, Lochaweside, Dalmally, T01838-200256, www.loch-awe.com/inistrynich. This delightful cottage (sleeps 4-8) is nestled by the loch. Fishing, golf and walking nearby.

Inveraray and around *p43*
££££ Crinan Hotel, T01546-830261, www.crinanhotel.com. Nestled on the shores of Loch Crinan and by the famous Crinan Canal, guests are assured of fine dining and luxury in this acclaimed retreat. Fantastic views, pampering on a majestic scale and a sensational restaurant make a stay here well worthwhile.
£££-££ Fernpoint Hotel, T01499-302111. Located just off the quayside, this grand hotel offers comfort (including whirlpool baths), and good value lunch (1300-1630) and evening (1800-2045) dining.

£££-££ George Hotel, Main St, T01499-302111, www.thegeorgehotel.co.uk. Enjoy genuine hospitality and tasty local produce (see Restaurants, below) in this atmospheric, late 18th-century hotel with cosy bar, real ales and a resident ghost. The Merchants Room with double jacuzzi is booked up to 12 months in advance.
£ Inveraray Youth Hostel, Dalmally Rd, T01499-302454. Open Apr-end Oct. The perfect budget base from which to explore the nearby castle and town.
£ Kilmartin Hotel, opposite the church in Kilmartin village, T01546-510250. Offers 4 en suite rooms. Handy, comfortable stop whilst exploring historic Kilmartin Glen.

Self-catering
The Paymaster's House, T01499-302003, www.paymastershouse.co.uk. A delightful 1780s dated option, oozing character and history in the heart of Inverary. From £90-165 per night.

Kintyre *p46*
There are at least 4 self-catering options run by the Heritage Trust on the island. Visit www.isle-of-gigha.co.uk for further details.
££££-£££ Stonefield Castle Hotel, 2 miles north of Tarbert, on the A82 to Lochgilphead, T01422-323200. This impressive 18th-century former castle home of the Campbells provides guests with comfort, eye-catching views of Loch Fyne and acres of garden to walk off the delicious 4-course dinner.
££ Gigha Hotel, Isle of Gigha, T01583-505254, www.isle-of-gigha.co.uk. Comfortable, friendly hotel with double/family rooms and some looking out over the sea. Good-value food including dinner (**££**). Non-residents can enjoy breakfast for £9.35.
££ Kilberry Inn, west of Tarbert on the B8024, T01880-770223, www.kilberryinn.com. 3 rooms. Open Easter-Oct and at weekends in the winter. Offers superb Scottish meat and seafood dishes (**£££-£**),and cosy

comforts including a roaring log fire. Has a glowing reputation for serving fabulous food, especially seafood and locally sourced beef and lamb that has won the restaurant plaudits by national newspaper food critics.

££-£ Post Office House, 5 mins from the ferry, Gigha, T01475-650100. B&B and self-catering option. Owners also run the Isle of Gigha post office and general store, and rent out bikes (£10 per day).

£ Rhu House, Tarbert, T01880-820231, Comfortable B&B looking out over west Loch Tarbert. Handy for Islay ferry.

Camping

Portban Holiday Park, Kilberry, Tarbert, T01880-770224. Majestic views towards Jura from the comfort of your tent.

Cowal Peninsula and the Clyde Coast
p49

££££-£££ An Lauchin, Tighnabruaich, T01700-811239. This elegant hotel with its own moorings boasts exquisite dining (**£££**), beautiful decor and many a fine dram in the snug bar.

££ Kames Hotel, Kames, T01700-811489. Offers 10 en suite rooms, terrific views down the Kyles and great food.

Self-catering

Cove Park, Rosneath Peninsula, Loch Long, T01436-850123, www.covepark.org. Very unusual and extremely restful place to stay, on the shore of Loch Long, 20 mins by car from Helensburgh. Accommodation in one of 2 'pods' or 3 'cubes'. The former are designed to blend in seamlessly with the surrounding landscape, with balconies overlooking the loch, and can sleep up to 4 in 2 en suite bedrooms; £100 per pod per night (minimum 2 nights). The 'cubes' are designed for singles or couples and cost £40 per night each. If you're looking for something a bit different, or just to get away from it all, this is the place to come. It is also a centre for the creative arts and runs an annual programme of artists' residences. Recommended.

Camping

Glendaruel Caravan/Campsite, T01369-820267. Terrific secluded location, well maintained and close to amenities.

Isle of Bute *p51, map p51*

££££-£££ Balmory Hall, 3 miles south of Rothesay, at Ascog, T01700-500669, www.balmoryhall.com. This Italianate mansion, set in 10 acres of grounds and once home to the 3rd Marquess of Bute, is now a superior guesthouse run by Tony and Beryl. A stay here is a memorable experience, the setting is idyllic and the suites are elegant and sumptuous (sample the Bute Suite for some serious indulgence). The 7-course breakfast is an event in itself. There are also self-catering apartments for weekend breaks (£235 per person).

££ Kingarth Hotel, Kingarth, in the south of the island, T01700-831662, www.kingarth hotel.co.uk. Quiet, cosy 1782 inn offering genuine hospitality, terrific seafood or steak platters (**££-£**) and the chance to banter with the locals. A wonderful place to enjoy the food and ambience.

££-£ Cannon House Hotel, Battery Pl, Rothesay, T01700-502819. A comfortable Georgian townhouse. Close to the ferry.

Self-catering

Ardencraig House, Ardencraig Rd, Rothesay. T01700-505077. Luxury 4-apartment option in converted Victorian-era mansion with views of Clyde (£195-495 per week).

---

❼ Restaurants

Inveraray and around *p43*

£££-££ Loch Fyne Oyster Bar, at Cairndow on the A83 near Clachan, T01499-600482. Open daily from 0900. Book ahead at this famous seafood restaurant known to attract heavyweight (in both senses of the word) politicians and gastronomes alike. All the seafood is from sustainable stock. There's also an excellent delicatessen to further tempt your taste-buds, though doubt you'll have room after gorging on a seafood platter.

££-£ The George Hotel, Main St, T01499-302111. Real ales on tap, hearty bar meals and reasonably priced dinners using locally sourced meats and seafood. If staying, try the home-made jams.

££-£ Kilmartin House (Glebe Cairn) Café, Kilmartin Hotel, see Where to stay, above. Daily 1000-1700 and Thu-Sat evenings for dinner. Superb cooking, much better than you should expect, and a lesson to many other visitor attractions in how to do things well. Wholesome and healthy soups, snacks, home-made bread and excellent coffee. Book ahead if planning on dinner.

Cowal Peninsula and the Clyde Coast
p49

£££-££ An Lauchin, T01700-811239. Game terrine, venison with red onion marmalade, cranachan. Provide Scottish cuisine at its best.
£££-££ Inver Cottage, Strathlachlan on B8000, past Strachur, T01369-860537. Mouth-watering starters, succulent game and hand-dived scallops, to-die-for desserts and homely ambience. A gem so book ahead. Recommended.

Isle of Bute *p51, map p51*
£ West End Café, 1-3 Gallowgate, Rothesay, T01700-503596. Open Tue-Sun. It is a must while you are on Bute to sample the fish and chips at this award-winning chippy. Phone ahead to avoid the massive queues in summer.

Kintyre *p46*
Aug Mull of Kintyre Music Festival. If you're around Campbeltown in mid-Aug don't miss 3 days of the best in traditional Celtic music.
Sep Gigha Music Festival, held early in the month.

Cowal Peninsula and the Clyde Coast
p49
Aug Cowal Highland Gathering, held on the last weekend of the month. The world's largest and culminate in a

spectacular march of massed pipes and drums through the streets.
Oct Cowalfest. An action-packed week-long walking and arts festival in early Oct.

Isle of Bute *p51, map p51*
May Isle of Bute Jazz Festival, held during the May Bank Holiday weekend.
Jul Isle of Bute Dunoon Sheepdog Trials and Inverary Highland Games.

Loch Awe and Loch Etive *p41*
Boat trips
Loch Etive Cruises, T01866-822430. Cruises depart at 1000 and 1200 (2-hr cruise, £10) and 1400 (3-hr cruise; £15), Easter-Oct Sun-Fri (Sat, charters only). No booking necessary but arrive in plenty of time. The departure point is 1 mile from Taynuilt up the road to the Bonawe Heritage Site.

Fishing
Lochawe Boats, Arbrecknish by Dalavich, off the B840, T01866-833256. All year. £20 per day for rowing boat or canoe. £40 per day for outboard boat. Loch Awe fishing permits from £10 per day.

Inverary and around *p43*
Adventure and horse riding
Argyll Riding, Dalchenna Farm, 2 miles south of Inveraray on A83, T01499-302611, www.horserides.co.uk. BHS-approved riding school offering trekking (Easter-Oct). Also bungee trampolines, climbing walls and clay-pigeon shooting (daily from 1000).
Argyll Trail Riding, Brenfield Farm, Ardrishaig, T01546-603274, www.brenfield. co.uk. Riding trails or beach gallops from a ½-day to a full week, including 'Day Pub Trails' and the week-long Rob Roy Trail. Also clay-pigeon shooting.
Highland Horse Riding, Tarbert, Argyll, T01880-820333. Located just off the A83 past the southern end of Tarbert. Rides and hacks from 1 hr to a day. Instructional rides from age 8.

Boat trips

Craignish Cruises, Ardfern by Lochgilphead, T0845-3979824, T07747-023038. Aboard the 33-ft-long *Sea Leopard*, you'll explore the sealife rich waters of the Firth of Lorn and out to the islands and Corryvreckan. Tours from 2 hr (£20) to 4 hrs (£35). Skipper also offers boat as a water taxi to help cyclists and walkers reach remote locations. Price dependent on route.

Sanda Island, T01586-551987. Summer sailings (£25) from Campbeltown run daily. Spend 3 hrs on the privately owned historic island of Sanda (2 miles off Mull of Kintyre) with its cosy wee pub and ancient sites. Reached aboard the *Seren Las*. There are 6 self-catering cottages (from £360 per week) and a pub serving good food – **The Byron Darnton** – named after the largest ship to be wrecked on off the island in 1946.

⊖ Transport

Inverary and around *p43*

Bus There are buses from **Lochgilphead** to **Cairnbaan**, **Crinan**, **Achnamara** and **Tayvallich**, several times daily Mon-Fri, T01546-870330. There is at least 1 daily bus to **Oban** via **Kilmartin** (Mon-Sat) and several daily buses to **Inveraray**. There's a regular service to **Ardrishaig** and from Argyll to **Glasgow**.

Cycle hire Crinan Cycles, 34 Argyll St, Lochgilphead, T01546-603511. Mon-Sat 0930-1730. Bikes for rent from £8, also parts and repairs and will advise on routes and provide maps.

Kintyre *p46*

Air There is at least 1 flight daily (35 mins), all year round to **Glasgow**.

Bus There are 5 buses a day daily from Campbeltown via **Machrihanish Saddell**, 25 mins; **Carradale**, 45 mins; and to **Southend**, 25 mins. Ask at TIC for an *Area Transport Guide*.

Ferry There is a car and passenger ferry from **Portavadie** on the Cowal Peninsula to **Tarbert**, daily every hr Apr-Oct, 25 mins, £3.30 per passenger, £14.95 per car, less frequent departures in winter.

There are 9 daily ferries to **Lochranza** (Arran) and **Claonaig** on the west coast of Kintyre (and east of Kennacraig), 30 mins, £4.75 per passenger, £21.20 per car. Ferries leave from **Kennacraig**, 5 miles south of Tarbert, to to **Colonsay** (see page 80) and **Islay** (see page 85).

A small car and passenger ferry leaves from **Tayinloan** to the ferry pier at Ardminish on **Gigha**, Mon-Sat 0800-1800, Sun 1100-1700, 20 mins, £5.70 return per passenger, £21.10 per car.

Cowal Peninsula and the Clyde Coast *p49*

Bus West Coast Motors, T01586-552319, run 3 (No 386) buses Mon-Sat from the **Dunoon** ferry terminal to **Inveraray** via **Benmore Gardens**, **Strachur** and **Cairndow**. The 1st bus leaves at 0850. Alternatively, there are at least 5 buses daily (No 484) Mon-Sat from Dunoon ferry terminal to Lochgoilhead.

To reach the **CalMac** ferry at Portavadie for the CalMac ferry to Tarbert in mid Argyll, at least 1 bus (No 478) runs Mon-Sat from Dunoon to **Portavadie** ferry terminal via **Tighnabruaich** and **Kames**. The buses leaves Dunoon at 0711 and 1325.

To reach **Bute** from *Cowal* there's 1 bus (No 479) Wed and Fri, 2 on Sat and 3 on Sun from **Dunoon** to the CalMac ferry at **Colintraive**, where on reaching **Rhubodach** (Bute) the bus continues into **Rothesay**, 1 hr 40 mins.

Isle of Bute *p51, map p51*

Bus and ferry To cross from **Rothesay** to **Dunoon** on the Cowal Peninsula using the bus and ferry, there's at least 1 service (No 477) Mon-Sat. This bus travels to the ferry terminal at Rhubodach and on crossing, stops in Kames and Tighnabruaich before Dunoon, 1 hr 40 mins.

Isle of Arran

In the wedge of sea between Ayrshire and Kintyre lies the oval-shaped, compact Isle of Arran. A land of beauty and contrast, the rugged, mountainous north is akin in hue and character to the northwest Highlands, whilst the fertile, forested south is lowland country. Unspoiled and alive with ancient history, myths and geological treasures, 25-mile-long Arran deserves its sobriquet, 'Scotland in Miniature'. Moreover, despite its popularity and accessibility from the Central Belt, outside Brodick you're as likely to spot a deer as a fellow tourist.

Arriving on the Isle of Arran → *Phone code 01770.*

Getting there The main ferry route to Arran is from the distinctly unappealing Ayrshire town of Ardrossan to the island's main town, Brodick. **CalMac** ① *T0800-665000, www. calmac.co.uk,* car and passenger ferry makes the 55-minute journey Monday to Sunday. The journey costs £5.95 one-way per passenger, £43.50 one-way per car (cheaper in winter). The other ferry route is from Claonaig to Lochranza in the north of the island. The non-bookable car and passenger ferry makes the 30-minute trip seven to nine times daily during the summer (April to October), and there's one daily service in winter to Tarbert. The journey costs £5.40 per passenger and £23.85 per car (cheaper in winter); check the website for ferry times. There's a regular train connections from Glasgow Central. By car, from the south the main route to Arran is from the M74 motorway, on to the A71 via Kilmarnock, to Irvine and Ardrossan. ►► *See Transport, page 63.*

Getting around A reliable bus network makes using public transport feasible, although many visitors explore by bike. It is possible to cycle a full circuit of the island in one day. Once on the island, there are regular daily buses from Brodick to Blackwaterfoot via 'The String'; to Lamlash and Whiting Bay and on to Blackwaterfoot; to Corrie, Sannox, Lochranza, Catacol, Pirnmill, Machrie and Blackwaterfoot. Kildonan, Whiting Bay and back to Brodick.

Tourist information The **Brodick TIC** ① *T01770-303774, www.ayrshire-arran.com, Easter-Oct Mon-Fri 0900-1700, Sat 0900-1930), Sun 1000-1700, winter hours vary but are currently Mon-Sat 1000-1700,* is beside the pier and bus terminal.

Brodick

Whether coming to play golf (there are seven courses), walk, climb or sample the ales, whisky and cheese produced by proud Arranachs, the largest town and port of Brodick is where most visitors step ashore. Lying in a 'broad bay', (hence its Norse name *breidr vik*), Brodick offers up guesthouses, eateries and shops but little of the scenic charm that awaits along the outlying winding roads.

Two miles north of town and overlooking Brodick Bay is the impressive **Brodick Castle** ① *T01770-302202, castle and restaurant, Easter-Oct daily 1100-1600 (castle closes 1500 in*

Oct), walled garden 1000-1630, country park open all year, daily 0930-sunset; castle, garden and country park £11, concessions £8. The ancient seat of the Dukes of Hamilton, it is now a flagship NTS property. Parts of the castle date from the 13th century and extensions were added in the 16th, 17th and 19th centuries. With paintings, antiques and (apparently) ghosts aplenty, it's worth exploring the sumptuously furnished rooms and the walled garden. The surrounding country park has 11 miles of marked trails and an adventure playground.

Halfway between the village and the castle is the excellent **Arran Heritage Museum** ⓘ *T01770-302636, www.arranmuseum.co.uk, Apr-Oct daily 1030-1630, £3, concessions £2, children £1.50, family (children under 16) £7.* Within a former croft and smiddy, visitors can discover a wealth of information about the island's archaeology, geology and social history before popping next door to Café Rosaburn (April to October).

Just over a mile north you'll find **Arran Aromatics**, where nature has been harvested to produce handmade soaps and oils. Continuing to Cladach by the castle, there's the chance to undertake a 45-minute sampling tour of real ales including a tasty Arran Blonde at the

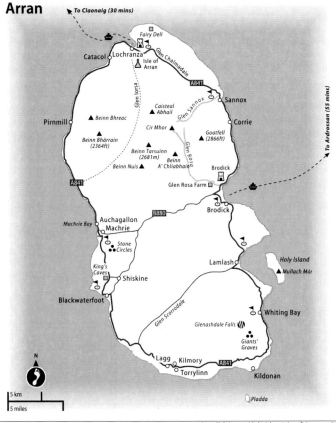

Arran

Arran Brewery ① T01770-302353, Easter-Oct Mon-Sat 1000-1700, Sun 1230-1700, Nov-Mar Mon-Sat 1000-1500, £2.50 guided tour (by arrangement), self-guided tour £2, children free.

South Arran

The south of Arran is a fertile landscape of rolling hills and pretty little seaside villages, where you'll find the bulk of the island's population and tourists. A few miles south of Brodick is **Lamlash**, a quiet and attractive village boasting a wide, sheltered bay but also an unappealing mud beach.

Lying just offshore is humpbacked **Holy Island** ① www.holyisland.org. Owned by Buddhists since 1992 they have established a meditative retreat and a peace centre (see Where to stay, page 62) on slopes grazed by feral goats and countless rabbits. A ferry runs to Holy Island between April and September, with a limited service in winter (£11 return). For further information on getting to Holy Island, call T01770-600998. For day visitors, there's just enough time to ascend **Mullach Mór** (1030 ft).

Renowned for its golf, the little fishing village of **Blackwaterfoot** is set round a bay with a tiny harbour. Two miles (45 minutes' walk) north along the coast are the **King's Caves**, where, according to legend, Robert the Bruce watched the spider that inspired him. The cathedral-like main cave has an unlocked iron gate to keep out sheep.

Four miles north of Blackwaterfoot, off the main coast road, is **Machrie Moor**, site of the most impressive of Arran's Bronze Age **stone circles**. Park by the Historic Scotland sign and then walk for 1.5 miles up the farm track to reach an area boasting six stone circles. Many are barely visible above the ground, but the tallest is over 18 ft high. A few miles further on, just south of the turn-off to Machrie village, is another Historic Scotland sign for **Moss Farm Road Stone Circle**, which lies about half a mile walk along the farm track.

North Arran

The northern half of Arran, with its wild, heather-strewn hillsides, brooding glens and dramatic mountains, contrasts sharply with the south. Sparsely populated, this remote region is paradise for the dedicated hillwalker. Six miles north of Brodick is the quaint village of **Corrie**. In addition to its craftshop, hotel and friendly pub, Corrie is also an alternative start-point to Brodick for the ascent of Goatfell. The main coastal road continues north from Corrie to **Sannox**, with its sandy beach and fine hotel before winding northwest into the heather-strewn glen and dropping into the former herring village of Lochranza.

Nestling under dramatic mountains and reached by road or the ferry from Claonaig, Arran's most northerly village of **Lochranza** is dominated by the ruins of 13th-century **Lochranza Castle** and the seal rich, U-shaped bay in which it stands. If the herds of deer grazing on the golf course contribute to Lochranza's air of serenity, the Highland atmosphere is accentuated by the presence of **Isle of Arran Distillery** ① T01770-830264, www.arranwhisky.com, Mar-Oct daily 1000-1800, Sun 1100-1800, call for winter opening hours, informative 1-hr guided tours cost £4.50, concessions £3.50. Opened in 1995, it's the island's first legal whisky distillery for over 170 years.

Walks on Arran → OS map No 69 covers these walks.

Arran is paradise for the outdoor enthusiast, offering a variety of forest, hilltop and coastal walks. There's even a 60-mile circuitous island route called the **Arran Coast Way** ① www.coastalway.co.uk. The north part of the island boasts ten peaks of over 2000 ft and several challenging ridge walks while the gentler south features less strenuous forest walks. Note all mountain routes should only be undertaken in good weather, whilst some – **A'Chir**,

Witches Step, **Suidhe Fherghas** and **Cioch Na Oighe** – involve scrambling and can be very dangerous for the inexperienced and unprepared. In all cases, good OS maps (and ropes) are available from the TIC office in Brodick. Local advice must be sought before venturing onto the hills during the deer-stalking season (August to October).

The **Glenashdale Falls and Giants' Graves walk** is one of the most popular in south. It's a steady, easy climb through woodland with the considerable incentive of a beautiful waterfall at the end of it. Both walks can be done together and should take around two to three hours in total, though you should allow some time to enjoy the falls. If you want to take a picnic, pop into the village shop which has a wide range of deli-type foods and local cheeses. The trail starts by the bridge over **Glenashdale Burn**. There's a map board here showing the route. Walk up the track alongside the burn until you see the sign for the path leading to the left up to the **Giants' Graves**. It's about 40 to 45 minutes up to the graves and back to this point, but it's a stiff climb up a steep staircase of 265 steps. At the top continue left along a path through the trees, which then curves right until you reach a clearing and the graves, which are chambered tombs, believed to be around 5000 years old. Depending on the light, this can be a very eerie, but almost magical place. Return back down the steps, and head left along the main path as it climbs steadily above the burn, past smaller falls, until you reach the main falls. The setting is stunning and the falls are spectacular as they plummet 140 ft into the pools below. You can rest and have a picnic at the top of the falls, or follow the paths down to the pools below which you can swim. The path back down to **Whiting Bay** passes the scant remains of an Iron Age fort, then turns back uphill to reach a broad track. Turn right, cross a small burn by stepping stones, then follow the track downhill all the way to the main road, a short way along from the car park.

Arran's most popular peak, **Goatfell**, is also its highest, at 2866 ft. There's a path leading up from Corrie, but most people begin the walk from the car park at Cladach sawmill, near Brodick Castle. The path is well marked and, apart from the final section, relatively easy. It runs initially through the **Brodick Country Park**, then follows the Cnocan burn as it rises steadily through woodland before crossing the Mill burn. Beyond the burn is a deer fence above which the landscape changes to heather moorland and the path begins to climb the flanks of the mountain. The final 650 ft up to the top is steep and rocky though the path is clear even when undertaking a gentle scramble on loose scree. Hopefully, your climb will be rewarded with spectacular views down the Firth of Clyde, over Arran's ridges and westwards towards Islay and Jura. In total the walk should take about five hours. Despite the hordes of walkers, treat this ascent with the same caution and respect as on any Scottish mountain. Certainly, the adjacent ridges should only be attempted by experienced hill-goers. In all instances, you should be dressed and equipped appropriately and be prepared for any sudden change in the weather.

Many of the walks start from Glen Rosa Farm. One of these takes in the three Beinns; **Beinn Nuis**, **Beinn Tarsuinn** (2681 ft) and **Beinn A'Chliabhain**. Start at Glen Rosa Farm and go up the Wood Road to the High Deer Gate, then to Torr Breac and the 'Y' junction at the top of the Garbhalt and on to the path which runs round the Three Beinns. This is a full day's walk.

Another excellent walk is from Glen Rosa to the head of the Glen; then take the path up into the Coire Buidhe and on to the ridge between **Cir Mhor** (2617 ft) and **A'Chir** (known as the Ceems Ridge). Then follow the path around the west side of A'Chir. This is not easy to find, but takes you around the back of A'Chir to Bowman's Pass and the north end of Beinn Tarsuinn. From here take the path to Beinn A'Chliabhan and down to the foot of Garbhalt Ridge and back down to Glen Rosa.

Cir Mhor can also be climbed from Glen Rosa. Before going over into Glen Sannox take the steep path straight up. On the way back down, head into Coire Buidhe and back down the glen. You can also continue from the top of Cir Mhor and take the path around the west side of A'Chir to the north end of the Bowman's Pass up on to Beinn Tarsuinn and along the ridge to Beinn Nuis, then down the path to the Garbhalt Bridge.

Finally, in **Lochranza** there's an easy two-hour coastal walk from the youth hostel along the north shore of Lochranza Bay (Newton Shore) to the viewpoint at Kirn Point affording lovely views down the Kilbrannan Sound. A mile northwards, past the geological phenomenon known as Hutton's unconformity is the rustic cottage of 'Fairy Dell' above which a track briefly climbs and leads back to North Newton and past the creative croft at The Whins where artist Reg assembles and sells his delightfully quirky 'stone-men'.

There are also several walks in and around **Glen Sannox**. It's a pleasant walk just to make your way up the head of the Glen and return the same way. You can walk up the Glen to beyond the old mine then make your way up towards the Devil's Punchbowl until you reach the main path and follow that down into the Coire. Take the main path back down into Glen Sannox instead of trying to climb out of the Devil's Punchbowl. You can also walk from Glen Sannox to Glen Rosa, which takes around four hours.

Isle of Arran listings

For hotel and restaurant price codes and other relevant information, see pages 13-20.

● Where to stay

Brodick p58

££££ Kilmichael Country House Hotel, T01770-302219, www.kilmichael.com. Take the road towards the castle, turn left at the golf course and follow the signs. Enjoy refined elegance in the island's oldest house. Their restaurant is the best on the island. Booking is essential for non-residents. No children under 12.

££££-£££ Auchrannie Country House Hotel, just beyond the turning to Kilmichael, T01770-302234, www.auchrannie.co.uk. Superb child-friendly facilities, and also has a 36-bedroom spa resort. Their Eighteen 69 (**££**) is highly rated and Brambles Bistro serves bar meals. Self-catering available. Very popular.

££ Belvedere Guest House, T01770-302397. Friendly guesthouse combining B&B with complimentary reiki or aromatherapy.

Camping

Glen Rosa, 2 miles from town on the road to Blackwaterfoot, T01770-302380, www.glenrosa.com. Open Apr-Oct. Fairly basic but beautifully situated campsite.

South Arran p60

££ Eden Lodge Hotel, Whiting Bay, T01770-700357, www.edenlodgehotel.co.uk. Friendly, with home-cooking and a beer garden.

££-£ Holy Isle Peace Centre, T01770-601100, www.holyisland.org. Comfortable rooms and 3 vegetarian meals a day form part of relaxing experience on this Buddhist-run isle.

North Arran p60

£ Castlekirk, Lochranza, T01770-830202, www.castlekirk.co.uk. Pleasant B&B in a converted church with views of the castle.

£ Lochranza SYHA, Lochranza, T08701-553255, T01770-830631. Open Feb-Oct. Friendly hostel with views over the bay.

Self-catering

Butt Lodge, T01770-302303, www.buttlodge.com. Secluded, luxury house with hinoki hot-tub. £1200-1700 per week.

Camping
Campsite next to the golf course near the **Arran Distillery**, Lochranza, T01770-820273, www.lochranzagolf.com. Open Apr-Oct.

🍴 Restaurants

Brodick *p58*
£££-££ Creelers Seafood Restaurant, Home Farm, near the castle, T01770-302797, www.creelers.co.uk. Excellent seafood, game and vegetarian dishes.
££-£ Café Rosaburn, by Heritage Museum, T01770-302636. Delicious, freshly made salads and home-cooking in a converted croft.

North Arran *p60*
££ Catacol Bay Hotel, Catacol, T01770-830231, www.catacol.co.uk. Hearty meals 1200-2200, Sun buffet popular with the islanders.
££ Isle of Arran Distillery, T01770-830264. Apr-Oct Mon-Sat 1000-1800, Sun 1100-1800, call for winter or evening opening hours. Locally sourced produce.

⚙ What to do

Brodick *p58*
Arran Adventure, T01770-302244, www.arranadventure.com. Hire a bike here from £6. Also offer sea kayaking, climbing, abseiling, archery and gorge walking.
Flying Fever, Strathwhillan Farm, Cottage 2, Strathwillan Rd, T01770-303899, T07717-712727 (mob), www.flyingfever.net. May-Oct. Quad-bike at Balmichael and paraglide. Offers a tandem flight as part of a Funday for £100.

North Arran *p60*
North Sannox Pony Trekking Centre, T01770-810222. Mon-Sat. £18 for a 1-hr trek.

🚍 Transport

Brodick *p58*
Bus Bus to **Lochranza** connects with the **Claonaig ferry** or to **Brodick** for the ferry to **Ardossan**.

Car hire Arran Transport, at Brodick pier, T01770-302121. Car hire from £25.

Ferry The main ferry route is to **Ardrossan** from **Brodick**. CalMac ferry, 55-mins.
The other route is to **Claonaig** from **Lochranza** in the north of the island. A non-bookable car/passenger ferry, 30 mins, for times, T0800-665000, www.calmac.co.uk.

🛈 Directory

Brodick *p58*
Banks Brodick has banks with ATMs, but these are the only ones on the island.
Post Post office, opposite the pharmacy.

Mull and Iona

Whether bathed in sunshine or shrouded in mist, each of Scotland's isles possess a magical quality. The Isle of Mull, a 50-minute sail from Oban and the third largest of the Hebridean islands, is no different. Teeming with wildlife and a gateway to the tiny and spiritual isle of Iona, Mull (derived from the Norse meaning 'high, bold headland') supports 2800 inhabitants and remains one of Scotland's most popular Hebridean isles. Indeed, Mull, just 26 miles east to west and 24 miles north to south, has enough going for it to appeal to most tastes: spectacular mountain scenery, 300 miles of wild coastline, castles, a narrow-gauge railway, fine cuisine and, in Tobermory, one of Scotland's prettiest coastal villages that also served as the main setting for the cult children's TV series, *Balamory*.

Visiting Mull and Iona

Getting there and around Mull is served by regular car/passenger ferry services, mostly from Oban but also from Kilchoan on the Ardnamurchan Peninsula and Lochaline on the Morvern Peninsula. Once on the island you can get to most places by bus. Services given in the Transport section are for April to October. Winter services are less frequent. There are regular five-minute sailings from Iona. ▸▸ *See Transport, page 77.*

Tourist information The **Craignure TIC** ⓘ *T01680-812377, open all year daily*, is opposite the pier in the same building as the **CalMac** office. **Tobermory TIC** ⓘ *at the far end of Main St, T01688-302182, Apr-Sep*, is also in the same building as the **CalMac** office.

Mull → *For listings, see pages 74-77.*

Arriving in Mull

For bus times, contact the operators listed under Transport, or ideally pick up the comprehensive *Mull Area Transport Guide* at the tourist offices in Oban, Tobermory or Craignure. This also includes ferry times.

Craignure to Tobermory

The arrival point for visitors is the village of Craignure. One and a half miles south of here is **Torosay Castle and Gardens** ⓘ *T01680-812421, Apr to mid-Oct daily 1030-1700, £7, concession £6, children £4*, more of a baronial family home than a full-blown castle. The best way to arrive is by the **Mull and West Highland Railway** ⓘ *T01680-812494, Easter to Oct 1100-1700, £5, children £3.50 return*, affectionately known as the *Balamory Express*.

A couple of miles east of Torosay is **Duart Castle** ⓘ *T01680-812309, Apr Sun-Thu 1000-1600, May to mid-Oct daily 1030-1730, £5.50, concessions £4.80, children £2.65*. The 13th-century ancestral seat of the Clan Maclean stands imperiously at the end of a promontory, commanding impressive views over Loch Linnhe and the Sound of Mull. Every five years (the next is in 2017) the castle and Mull hosts the Clan Maclean Gathering. The castle's main feature is the tower house, built in the late 14th century when it became the main residence of the Macleans of Duart. Today it's a fascinating place to visit, with many relics and artefacts on display.

Midway between Craignure and Tobermory, on the main A849, is the pretty village of **Salen**, where a fantastic culinary experience awaits at **Mediterranea** (see Restaurants, page 75). Salen, situated at the narrowest point on the island, has several sites of interest on its doorstep. Two miles south is Mull's tiny and only airfield, adjacent to which is the excellent **Glenforsa Hotel** (see Where to stay, page 74) where majestic views down the Sound of Mull can also be enjoyed. One mile north of Salen, overlooking the bay, is the ruin of **Aros Castle**, built in the 14th century and one of the strongholds of the Lords of the Isles. Tradition holds that the treasure of the Spanish galleon sunk in Tobermory Bay in 1588, was recovered by the Macleans and lies buried beneath Aros Castle.

Four miles southwest of Salen, near Gruline and Loch Ba, is the **MacQuarrie Mausoleum**, which houses the remains of Major-General Lachlan MacQuarrie (1761-1824). He took over as Governor-General of New South Wales from the unpopular William Bligh, formerly of the *Bounty*, and became known as the 'Father of Australia'. The mausoleum is maintained by the NTS, on behalf of the National Trust of Australia.

Mull

Tobermory

There is surely no prettier port in the west of Scotland than Tobermory, Mull's main village and setting for most of the popular children's TV series *Balamory*. Followers of the now-defunct series should ask for the Balamory leaflet at the TIC office, which highlights the key

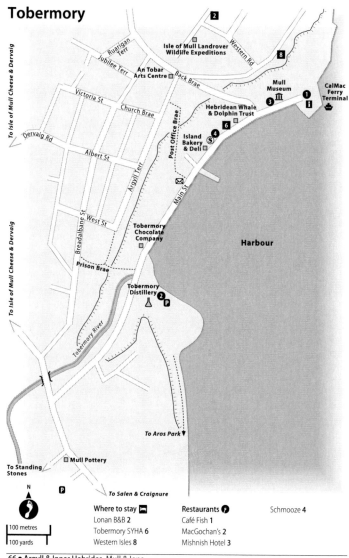

Tobermory

Where to stay 🛏️
Lonan B&B **2**
Tobermory SYHA **6**
Western Isles **8**

Restaurants 🍴
Café Fish **1**
MacGochan's **2**
Mishnish Hotel **3**

Schmooze **4**

filming locations. Tobermory got its name from a small settlement once situated northwest of the current village where there's a spring known in Gaelic as Tobar (well) Mhoire (Mary). The brightly painted houses that line Tobermory's harbour front date from the late 18th century when the British Fisheries Society built Tobermory as a planned herring port. During the Second World War, as a naval training base Tobermory was euphemistically called HMS Western Isles. Nowadays, only a few fishing boats, but dozens of yachts, bob at anchor in the protected waters of the natural harbour. Lying at the bottom of the harbour is a galleon of the Spanish Armada, which sank in mysterious circumstances, along with its treasure of gold doubloons. Remnants of a Spanish galleon can be seen on Main Street in the wonderful **Mull Museum** ① *T01688-301100, Easter-Oct Mon-Fri 1000-1600, £2*, housed in an old bakery. Raining or not, it's worth visiting to gleen an insight of the island's history.

The harbour front (Main Street) is where you'll find most of what you want: the tourist office, tours, hotels, guesthouses, restaurants, pubs and the award-winning baker. Mercifully, though, it's free from the tartan tat that blights so many other tourist hotspots. At the foot of the main road down to the harbour is the tiny **Tobermory Distillery** ① *T01688-302645, www.burnstewartdistillers.com, Mon-Fri 1000-1700, £3, concessions £1, children free*, which offers a guided tour rounded off with a sampling of the island's single malt. At the top of Back Brae, on Argyll Terrace, is **An Tobar** ① *T01688-302211, www.antobar.co.uk, Mon-Sat 1000-1600, Sun 1400-1700, free*, an excellent arts centre housed in the old school and featuring a varied programme of exhibitions, music and workshops. Or you can just have a coffee and cake by the fire and admire the view.

West coast Mull

Mull's west coast is where you'll find some of the island's most stunning scenery. The B8073 winds its way anti-clockwise from Tobermory in a series of twists and turns as it follows the contours of the coastline. The road climbs west from Tobermory then makes a dramatic descent, with hairpin bends, to Dervaig.

Dervaig is a lovely village of whitewashed cottages, beautifully situated at the head of Loch Cuin. Here sits **Kilmore Church**, with its unusual pencil-shaped spire. Until its closure in 2006, Dervaig was also the home of the smallest professional theatre in Britain. A fundraising campaign is helping to establish a new theatre south of Tobermory for the famous **Mull Touring Theatre Company** ① *T01688-302673*. One mile beyond Dervaig take the turn-off to Torloisk to reach Glen Bellart and the highly informative **Old Byre Heritage Centre** ① *T01688-400229, Easter-Oct Wed-Sun 1030-1830, £4, concessions £3, children £2*. In addition to a new geology exhibition there are dozens of exhibits and several films (including one for toddlers) that highlight the history of Mull through the ages and its varied wildlife. Ask about the location of the nearby Neolithic standing stones. The tea rooms delicious home-baking is an additional treat, see Restaurants, page 75.

Five miles west of Dervaig is **Calgary Bay**, Mull's most beautiful beach ringed by steep wooded slopes with views across to Coll and Tiree. Calgary in Alberta, Canada, was named after the former township. Many emigrants were forcibly shipped to Canada from here during the Clearances. There are some wonderful paths through Calgary Wood, just past **Calgary Farmhouse Hotel**, including a half-hour circular walk.

Isle of Ulva

If you have the time and need to escape the hectic bustle of Mull, then take a day out on idyllic Ulva (meaning 'wolf island' in Norse), just off the west coast. You won't see any wolves around, but you're almost guaranteed to spot deer, golden eagles, buzzards and seals offshore. There are several woodland and coastal trails across the island, including one to the southwest where there are basalt columns similar to those on Staffa. Alternatively, you can follow the trail to the top of the hill for views across to the Cuillins on Skye (on a clear day), or else cross the causeway to Ulva's even smaller neighbour **Gometra**. For more information on the island walks and on its history, visit the **Boathouse Heritage Centre** ① *a restored thatched croft house close to the ferry slip, T01688-500241, Easter-Oct Mon-Fri 0900-1700 and Sun Jun-Aug only, £5, children £2, entry is included in the ferry fare (see Transport, page 77)*. There's also a tea room where you can try the local oysters with Guinness. Note that there are no camping facilities on Ulva, but ask the ferryman for advice on possible places to wild camp.

Staffa

The tiny uninhabited island of Staffa, 5 miles off the west coast of Mull, is one of the most spectacular sights not just in Scotland but anywhere in the world. It consists of immense hexagonal, basalt pillars, which loom up out of the sea like a giant pipe organ. Staffa was formed 60 million years ago by the slow cooling of Tertiary basalt lavas. These have been carved by the pounding sea into huge cathedral-like caverns such as the mightily impressive **Fingal's Cave**. The sound of the sea crashing against the black crystalline columns made such an impression on Felix Mendelssohn in 1829 that he immortalized the island in his *Hebrides Overture*. The composer was obviously aware of its original name in Gaelic, which means 'The Melodious Cave'. You can land on the island – if the weather is good enough – and walk into the cave via the causeway; an experience not to be missed. But even if the seas are too rough, it's worth making the 90-minute boat trip just to witness the columns and cave.

South Mull

From Ulva Ferry the B8073 heads east along the north shore of **Loch na Keal** then enters a wide flat valley, where the road forks east to Salen and west along the south shore of Loch na Keal. This part of Mull is dominated by **Ben More** (3170 ft), the island's highest mountain. All around is a spectacular region of high jutting mountains and deep glens, extending west to the **Ardmeanach Peninsula**. The peninsula may look impenetrable, but with the proper walking gear can be explored on foot. On the north coast, about a mile from the road, is the massive entrance to **MacKinnon's Cave**, which runs for about 100 yds back under the cliffs. Make sure to visit only at low tide. The area around the headland, now owned by the National Trust for Scotland, is known as **The Wilderness**. Near the headland is **MacCulloch's Tree**, a fossilized tree 40 ft high and thought to be 50 million years old, which was discovered in 1819. The tree is only accessible by a 7-mile footpath which begins at Burg Farm. You should have a map of the area and also time your arrival with low tide.

Mull's southernmost peninsula stretches west for 20 miles from the head of Loch Scridain as far as Iona. Most visitors use it merely as a route to Iona but there are a couple of interesting little detours along the way. A twisting side road leads south from Pennyghael over the hills and down to **Carsaig Bay**, from where you can head east or west along the shore for some dramatic coastal scenery. Two roads lead south from Bunessan. One leads to **Scoor**, near where is a great beach at Kilveockan. The other road splits near the coast: the left branch leads to **Uisken Bay**; the right-hand branch leads to **Ardlanish Bay**, each with a good beach.

The road ends at **Fionnphort**, the departure point for the small passenger-only ferry to Iona, just a mile across the Sound of Iona. The village is little more than a car park, a row

Things to do on Mull when it's wet

It rains a lot on Mull, but luckily there's a fairly large number of indoor options to keep you nice and dry until the weather changes. If you've just arrived off the ferry from Oban and it's chucking it down, then head straight for **Torosay Castle** (page 64), just to the south of Craignure. And if the weather changes whilst exploring the interior, don't miss the gardens. Just beyond the castle is **Wings Over Mull**, a bird of prey conservation centre, which offers indoor hawk-handling and a chance to learn about the island's incredible bird life. Nearby is Mull's greatest fortification, **Duart Castle** (page 64), which is also worth a peek. If all that history gets too

much then you could do worse than hole up in the bar of the **Craignure Inn** (page 74) and relax in front of the roaring log fire.

In the north of the island, the most appealing option by far is the **Old Byre Heritage Centre** (page 67), not far from the picturesque village of Dervaig. When in Tobermory do as the locals do, and get yourself down to the **The Mish** bar, see Restaurants and Entertainment, page 75, though you shouldn't really need the excuse of inclement weather. Meanwhile, over in Fionnphort, the departure point for the pilgrimage to Iona, you can seek a wee dram in the cosy **Keel Row Bar**.

of houses, a pub and a shop, but there are several inexpensive B&Bs for those arriving too late to make the crossing. Even if you're not staying, it's worth stopping off in the village to visit the **Columba Centre** ① *Apr-Sep daily 1100-1700, free*, where interpretive displays tell the story of St Columba.

A road runs south from Fionnphort to **Knockvologan**, opposite **Erraid Island**, which is accessible at low tide. The island has literary connections, for it was here that Robert Louis Stevenson is believed to have written *Kidnapped*. **Balfour Bay** on the south of the island is named after the novel's hero who was shipwrecked here.

Walks on Mull → *OS Landranger maps 47, 48 and 49 cover the entire island.*
Mull presents numerous walking opportunities, ranging from gentle forest trails to wild and dramatic coastal routes, or even a spot of Munro-bagging for the more intrepid. With the exception of the Cuillins on Skye, Mull's highest peak, **Ben More** (3170 ft) is the only Munro not on the mainland.

The trail starts at a lay-by on the B8035, at Dishig, and is fairly clear, though it can be tricky near the top. Return the same way, or more experienced climbers could continue down the narrow ridge to the eastern summit, **A'Chioch**, then descend the eastern face to the road that skirts **Loch Ba**. The views from the top are magnificent, across the other Hebridean islands and even as far as Ireland. If it's a cloudy day, it's worth postponing the ascent until there's clear weather. Allow around six hours for the round trip.

There are a couple of excellent coastal walks which start out from Carsaig Bay. A good path heads west along the shore to **Carsaig Arches** at Malcom's Point. The path runs below the cliffs out to the headland and then around it, and after about a mile reaches **Nun's Cave**, a wide and shallow cave where the nuns of Iona took refuge after being expelled during the Reformation. The path continues for another mile or so, but becomes a bit exposed in places and traverses a steep slope above a sheer drop into the sea. The famous arches are columnar basalts worn into fantastic shapes. One is a free-standing rock stack and another is a huge cave with two entrances. You'll need to allow about four hours in total plus some time at the arches.

Heading east from Carsaig Bay is a spectacular 4½-mile walk to **Lochbuie**, past **Adnunan stack**. It starts out through woodland, then follows the shore below the steep cliffs, with waterfalls plunging straight into the sea. It's easy at first but then gets very muddy in places and there's quite a bit of wading through boggy marsh, so make sure you've got good walking boots. Allow about five to six hours in total.

A shorter walk takes you to the Bronze Age Lochbuie Stone Circle at the foot of **Ben Buie**. Leave your car at the stone bridge before you reach the village. Look for the green sign on the gate to your left and follow the white marker stones across the field. The stone circle is hidden behind a wall of rhododendrons, so follow the marker stones across the plank bridge until you see it. It takes about 30 minutes.

There are several marked trails through Forestry Commission land on Mull. The first walk is to **Aros Park**, on the south side of Tobermory Bay. Start out from the car park near the distillery in Tobermory and follow the shoreline for about a mile to Lochan a'Ghurrabain, which is good for trout fishing. From here there is also a marked path around the loch (1 mile). A longer walk is to **Ardmore Bay**, 3 miles north of Tobermory. The trail/cycle path starts at the car park by the road that runs northwest from Tobermory. From here, it runs out almost to Ardmore point and back again, passing a couple of ruined villages on the way. There's a good chance of seeing seals and sea birds in Ardmore Bay. The trail is 4 miles in total.

Four miles north of Craignure is the car park and picnic site at **Garmony Point**, where a 2-mile trail leads to the ferry terminal at **Fishnish**, hugging the shore all the way. Another trail (4 miles) runs out to Fishnish Point and back through the forest to the car park.

Iona → *For listings, see pages 74-77. Phone code 01681. Population 130.*

Iona is a small island – barely 3 miles long and a little over a mile wide – but its importance to Christianity is out of all proportion to its size. Iona's place in religious history was guaranteed when St Columba arrived in the land of the Gaels with his 12 disciples and founded a monastery there in AD 563. The Irish monk then set about converting a large part of pagan Scotland (for the head-hunting Picts to the north and east followed the teachings of Druids) and much of northern England. Iona went on to become the most sacred religious site in Europe and has been a place of pilgrimage for several centuries. Today that pilgrimage has turned into more of an invasion, with day-trippers making the five-minute ferry trip from Mull to visit the abbey. Few, however, venture beyond the main village, **Baile Mór**, and it's easy to find a quiet spot, particularly on the west coast with its sparkling silver beaches washed by turquoise sea. It's worth spending a day or two here to soak up the island's unique spiritual peace so well conveyed in the words of Dr Johnson: "that man is little to be envied whose … piety would not grow warmer among the ruins of Iona".

Background

Iona is known as the 'Cradle of Christianity in Scotland', and was once a centre of the arts. The monks produced elaborate carvings, manuscripts, ornate gravestones and Celtic crosses. Their greatest work was the beautiful *Book of Kells*, which dates from AD 800, and which is now on display in Dublin's Trinity College. This proved to be the high point of the church's history. Shortly after came the first of the Viking raids, in AD 806, when many monks were slaughtered at Martyrs' Bay, followed by another in AD 986 which destroyed the work of many years. The relentless pressure from the established church ended with the suppression of the Celtic Church by King David in 1144.

In 1203 Iona became part of the mainstream church with the establishment of a nunnery for the Order of the Black Nuns, as well as a Benedictine Abbey by Reginald of the MacDonalds of the Isles. Iona became overshadowed by the royal city of Dunfermline, and its final demise came with the Reformation when buildings were demolished and all but three of the 360 carved crosses destroyed.

The abbey lay in ruins until, in 1899, the island's owner, the eighth Duke of Argyll, donated the buildings to the Church of Scotland on condition that the abbey church was restored for worship. Then, in 1938, the Reverend George Macleod founded the Iona Community as an evangelical Church of Scotland 'brotherhood', with the abbey buildings

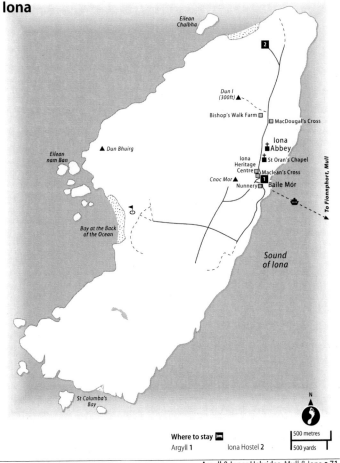

Iona

Eilean Chalbha

Eilean nam Ban

▲ Dun Bhuirg

Dun I (300ft) ▲

Bishop's Walk Farm ▣   ▣ MacDougal's Cross

Iona Abbey
■ St Oran's Chapel

Iona Heritage Centre ▣
▣ Maclean's Cross
Cnoc Mor ▲   **1** Baile Mór
Nunnery ▣

To Fionnphort, Mull

Bay at the Back of the Ocean

Sound of Iona

St Columba's Bay

N

Where to stay ▣
Argyll **1**   Iona Hostel **2**

500 metres
500 yards

The story of St Columba

St Columba (Colum Cille in Gaelic), a prince of Ireland and grandson of the Irish King, Niall of the Nine Hostages, came to Scotland not as a missionary, but as an act of self-imposed penance for his actions. He stubbornly refused to hand over his copy of the Gospels, illegally copied from St Finian's original, which led to a bitter dispute with the king. This ended in a pitched battle in which Columba's supporters prevailed, but he was so overcome with remorse at the bloodshed he had caused that he fled Ireland, finally settling on Iona as it was the first place he found from where he couldn't see his homeland. Columba, however, was not retiring into obscurity.

His missionary zeal drove him to begin building the abbey. He banished women and cows from the island, declaring that "where there is a cow there is a woman, and where there is a woman there is mischief". Workers at the abbey had to leave their womenfolk on nearby Eilean nam Ban (Women's Island). Not content with that, he also banished frogs and snakes from Iona, though there are plenty on Mull. He is even said to have pacified the Loch Ness Monster during a visit to Inverness. He went on to found the Celtic Church, or the Church of the Culdees, with centres throughout Scotland, which differed in many ways from the Church of Rome.

as its headquarters, and by 1965 had succeeded in rebuilding the remainder of the monastic buildings. Now the abbey complex has been completely restored and the island of Iona, apart from the abbey buildings, is owned by the National Trust for Scotland.

The abbey
ⓘ *Apr-Sep daily 0930-1730; Oct-Mar 0930-1630. £5.50, concessions £4.50, children £3.30.*
The present abbey dates from around 1200, though it has been rebuilt over the centuries and was completely restored in the 20th century. The oldest part is the restored **St Oran's Chapel**, to the south of the abbey on the right, which is plain and unadorned save for its splendid 11th-century Norman doorway. You get a good view of the whole complex from the top of the small grassy knoll opposite the abbey entrance. It is said that Columba was prevented from completing the building of the original chapel until a living person had been buried in the foundations. His friend Oran volunteered and was duly buried. Columba later asked for the face to be uncovered so that he could bid a final farewell to his friend, but Oran was found to be alive and claimed he had seen Heaven and Hell, describing them in such blasphemous terms that Columba ordered he be covered up immediately!

Surrounding the chapel is the **Reilig Odhrain**, the sacred burial ground, which is said to contain the graves of 48 Scottish kings, including Macbeth's victim, Duncan, as well as four Irish and eight Norwegian kings. The stones you see today are not the graves of kings but of various important people from around the West Highlands and Islands, including that of John Smith, leader of the British Labour Party from 1992 until his death in 1994.

Beside the Road of the Dead, which leads from the abbey church to St Oran's Chapel, stands the eighth-century **St Martin's Cross**. This is the finest of Iona's Celtic high crosses and is remarkably complete, with the Pictish serpent-and-boss decoration on one side and holy figures on the other. Standing in front of the abbey entrance is a replica of **St John's Cross**, the other great eighth-century monument. The restored original is in the Infirmary Museum, at the rear of the abbey, along with a fine collection of medieval gravestones.

No part of St Columba's original buildings survives, but to the left of the main entrance is **St Columba's Shrine**, the small, steep-roofed chamber which almost certainly marks the site of the saint's tomb. This is **Torr an Aba**, where Columba's cell is said to have been. The abbey itself has been carefully restored to its original beautiful simplicity and inside, in a side chapel, are marble effigies of the eighth Duke of Argyll and his third wife, Duchess Ina.

Baile Mór

The passenger ferry from Fionnphort on Mull lands at Baile Mór, Iona's main village, which is little more than a row of cottages facing the sea. There are over a dozen places to stay but, as demand far exceeds supply during the busy summer season, it's best to book in advance at one of the tourist offices on Mull or in Oban. There's also a post office, a very good craft shop and general store in the village. Just outside the village, on the way to the abbey, are the ruins of the **Augustinian nunnery**. To the north, housed in the parish church manse, built by Thomas Telford, is the **Iona Heritage Centre** ① *T01681-700576 Apr-Oct Mon-Sat 1030-1630, £2.20*, which features displays on the island's social history. Nearby stands the intricately carved 15th-century **Maclean's Cross**.

Around the island

On the west coast are some lovely beaches of white sand and colourful pebbles. The best of the lot is the **Bay at the Back of the Ocean**, beside the golf course, and only a 1½-mile walk from the ferry. This was one of John Smith's favourite places and it's easy to see why. At the southern tip of the island is another sandy beach at **St Columba's Bay**, believed to be the spot where the saint first landed. Another good walk is to the top of **Dun I**, the only real hill, which rises to a height of 300 ft. To get there, continue on the road north from the abbey, past MacDougal's Cross, then go through a gate to the right of Bishop's Walk Farm and follow the fence up to where you join a footpath up to the top. It's only about half an hour up and down and there are great views from the top of the entire island and the coastline of Mull.

Mull and Iona listings

For hotel and restaurant price codes and other relevant information, see pages 13-20.

😊 Where to stay

Craignure to Tobermory *p64*

££ Glenforsa Hotel, 2 miles south of Salen, T01680-300377. Open Easter-Oct. Delightful hotel run by friendly hotelier and aviator above whose reception hangs a propeller off a WWI aircraft. 27 tasteful, wood furnished rooms, beautiful views down the Sound of Mull and a lovely restaurant serving wild salmon, Mull oysters (**££**), and real ales.

££-£ Craignure Inn, Craignure, T01680-812305, www.craignure-inn.co.uk. This 18th-century inn, complete with an interior of rough hewn stone walls, wooden floor and some fire has an atmospheric cosy bar serving real ales and food that includes Hebridean lamb (**££-£**). Has 3 rooms available.

£ Arle Lodge, Aros, T01680-300299, www.arlelodge.co.uk. Friendly, independent hostel that offers continental breakfast as part of the deal.

£ Glenaros Lodge, Salen, T01680-300301, www.glenaroslodge.net. 18-bed hostel close to public transport between Craignure and Tobermory.

Camping

Balmeanach Park, Fishnish, T01680-300342. Well-equipped, child-friendly caravan and campsite.

Tobermory *p66, map p66*

£££-££ Western Isles Hotel, T01688-302012. Open all year. Owners Esplin Chapman and Richard Nealon are proud this grand, sandstone hotel with commanding views over Tobermory harbour is no longer part of a chain. Step inside and it's clear the pair are on a mission to transform this 23-room, Victorian-era hotel back to its former glory. The Master Seaview rooms are worth the additional pounds for the breathtaking view but whatever room you choose, expect great food and a warm welcome.

£ Lonan B&B, off Western Rd, T01688-302082. Open Easter-Oct. Welcoming, small B&B with lovely garden, terrific breakfasts and only 5 mins' walk from Main St.

£ Tobermory SYHA, Main St, T01668-302481. Terrific harbour-front location. Always busy so book ahead.

West coast Mull *p67*

££ Druimard Country House Hotel, Dervaig, T01688-400491, www.druimard.co.uk. Open end Mar-Oct. 6 tastefully furnished rooms with views to Glen Bellart. Good breakfast and can arrange wildlife and island tours.

£ Dervaig Bunkhouse, 6 miles from Tobermory, in tiny Dervaig, T01688-400249. A terrific budget option.

South Mull *p68*

£££ Pennyghael Hotel, in Pennyghael, overlooking the loch, T01681-704288, www.pennyghaelhotel.com. Serving locally farmed meats and seafood in the restaurant and a 4-course set dinner (**£££-££**). 2 self-catering cottages in the grounds from £375 per week.

Iona *p70, map p71*

£££-££ Argyll Hotel, T01681-700334, www.argyllhoteliona.co.uk. Open Apr-Oct. This remains the better of the island's 2 upmarket hotels with 17 rooms, a good restaurant and tours organized.

£ Iona Hostel, T01681-700781, www.ionahostel.co.uk. A fabulous hostel with views to the Treshnish Islands. 25-min walk north from the village and ferry. It's best to book ahead in summer. A wee gem of a hostel that also promises the best duck eggs this side of heaven.

🍴 Restaurants

Craignure to Tobermory *p64*
£££-££ Mediterranea, Salen, T01680-300200, www.mull-cuisine.co.uk. Open daily Tue-Sun and Fri, Sat 1830-2100, Sun 1100-1500 in the winter. An island gem serving Sicilian classics. Beyond the bright yellow door awaits mouth-watering seafood and pasta creations, delightful staff and a cosy ambience. Book ahead.

Tobermory *p66, map p66*
The best value fish and chips are sold nightly by the mobile vendor at the harbour front.
£££-£ Western Isles Hotel, see Where to stay, above. Tasty menu with local seafood and game on the finer dining room menu, or cheaper bar meals in the **Conservatory Bar**.
££ The Café Fish, right on the pier above the TIC, T01688-301253, www.thecafefish.com. Open Mon-Sat. Choose the cosy interior or al fresco for dining on the freshest seafood, including squat lobster. A real delight.
££ MacGochan's, T01688-302350, on the harbour front. Similar good pub grub and live music.
££-£ Mishnish Hotel, T01688-302009, Main St. Despite its makeover, 'the Mish' retains an element of charm and serves up hearty meals to accompany your real ale.
££-£ Shmooze Restaurant, Main St, T01688-302203. A welcome addition to the seafront, diners will find a frequently changing menu of seafood staples and an emphasis on freshly cooked Scottish fare. Reasonable value.

West coast Mull *p67*
££ Dovecote Restaurant, Calgary Hotel, by Dervaig, T01688-400256, www.calgary.co.uk. Open Mar-Nov. This is where to enjoy delicious fish and locally sourced meats in an informal atmosphere.
£ Old Byre Heritage Centre, Dervaig, see page 67. Open Apr-end Oct. Simple, home-made delights offered all day. Not a huge menu but a worthwhile lunch stop.

🎭 Entertainment

Mull *p64, map p65*
Mishnish Hotel, see Restaurants, above. Despite the 'themed' old-world decor it wins over **MacGochan's** for its ambience. Both pubs run live music events and attract a healthy numbers of revellers.
There are also music events at **An Tobar**, see page 67.

🎉 Festivals

Mull *p64, map p65*
Apr Mull Music Festival, known as the Whisky Olympics, for details T01688-302383. Held on the last weekend of the month, it is a great time to be on Mull. You can enjoy a feast of Gaelic folk music and, of course, whisky. The focus of the festival is the bar of the **Mishnish Hotel**, Tobermory.
Jul Mendelssohn on Mull Music Festival, held over 10 days in early Jul, is another great festival. It commemorates the famous composer's visit here in 1829. **Tobermory Highland Games**, is held annually on the 3rd Thu of the month.
Sep Mull and Iona Food Festival. This mid-Sep festival showcases the wealth of outstanding produce cultivated on the island.
Oct Tour of Mull Rally, held in early Oct for over 30 years. This should not be missed by rally enthusiasts, though book early as the island becomes extremely busy.

🛍 Shopping

Mull *p64, map p65*
From the local butcher and baker to the chocolate-maker, Tobermory is foodie-heaven. It's also where to pick up fishing tackle, camping and bike spares.
A Brown and Son Ironmonger, Main St, Tobermory, T01688-302020. First opened in 1897, this shop is now under new ownership but rest assured it has everything. In addition to trout-fishing permits, this is where to stock up on everything from

camping gas to tent pegs. They'll even change your watch battery.

Island Bakery and deli, Main St, T01688-302223. Try their award-winning organic lemon melts, oat crumbles and chocolate gingers with huge pieces of stem ginger.

Isle of Mull Cheese, on the edge of town, 500 yds off the Dervaig Rd, at Sgriob-Ruadh Farm, T01688-302235. Open Apr-Sep Mon-Fri 1000-1600. Here you can savour their award-winning, traditionally made cheese and admire their wonderful glass barn.

Mull Pottery, southern edge of Tobermory enroute to Salen, T01688-302347. Tasteful hand thrown pots in different shapes and sizes. Good café-bistro upstairs with views across Sound of Mull.

Tobermory Chocolate Company, Main St, T01688-302526. Open Mon-Sat 0930-1700, Sun 1000-1600. Here you can try out their speciality – chocolate made with the local whisky and delicious Staffa Cake.

⚙ What to do

Mull *p64, map p65*
Boat trips
Alternative Boat Hire, Mark Jardine, Sailing Trips & Boat Hire, Lovedale Cottage, T01681-700537, www.boattripsiona.com. Trips around the coastline and handline fishing on a traditional wooden boat. You can hire by the hour or for an afternoon, May-Oct, from Fionnphort and Iona.

Silver Swift, Raraig House, Raeric Rd, Tobermory, T01688-302390, www.tobermoryboatcharters.co.uk. Boat charter and wildlife cruises, £40, not recommended to children under 12. Spend a day cruising from Tobermory, passing Ardnamurchan lighthouse and spotting basking sharks and seals as you head for the island of Rùm. Picnic on the island before heading back. Trips run from Apr-Oct, call for days.

Turus Mara, Penmore Mill, Dervaig, T0800-858786, www.turusmara.com. Birdwatching and wildlife trips to Staffa, Iona and the Treshnish Isles costing from £25 (from Mull)

and £48 (from Oban). Chance to spot seals, puffins and visit the classic Fingal's Cave on Staffa. There's also a special day tour from Oban that includes visits to Ulva (Mull) and Staffa (£35).

Fishing
Sea Angling Trips, Tackle and Books, Main St, Tobermory, T01688-302336. Fish for mackerel, pollock and dogfish aboard *Amidas*. Trips last approximately 3 hrs and include equipment. £25, children £15. Min 6 people. The shop also sells trout fishing permits (from £5) for inland lochs. Ask the shop for its small leaflet with destinations. Also well stocked with walking maps and equipment.

Wildlife tours
You can find out about the sea-life around Mull by visiting the **Hebridean Whale and Dolphin Trust**, 28 Main St, Tobermory, T01688-302620, www.hwdt.org, Apr-Oct daily 1000-1700, Nov-Mar Mon-Fri 1100-1600. This charity aims to protect the marine environment through education.

Acclaimed wildlife documentaries have further fuelled demand for wildlife tours on the island. Visit www.wildisles.co.uk, for a list of operators.

Island Encounter Wildlife Safaris, Salen, T01680-300441, www.mullwildlife.co.uk. A full-day wildlife safari with local guide Richard Atkinson costs £37, including lunch. You'll see golden eagles, white-tailed sea eagles, hen harriers, divers, merlins, peregrine falcons, seals and porpoises, to name but a few.

Isle of Mull Land Rover Wildlife Expeditions, Ulva Ferry, T01688-500121, www.scotland wildlife.com. David Woodhouse runs these excellent day-long tours with lunch £42.50, children £39.50, and the chance to spot golden eagles, otters, seals and porpoise.

Sea Life Surveys, Ledaig, Tobermory, beside McGochan's pub, T01688-302916, www.sealifesurveys.com. Everything from whale, dolphin and shark-watching trips to gentle 'Ecocruz's' (£15) in sheltered waters to the full-day Whalewatch Explorer (£60) can be booked with this operator.

⊖ Transport

Craignure to Tobermory *p64*
Bus There are daily buses from **Craignure**, which coincide with ferry arrivals.

The **Craignure** to **Tobermory** via **Salen** service runs 6 times a day Mon-Fri, 4 times on Sat and 4 times on Sun, Bowman's Coaches, T01680-812313. There's a Bowmans bus from **Craignure** to **Fionnphort** (for Iona) 4 times a day Mon-Fri, 3 times on Sat and 1 on Sun.

Car Tobermory is a 30- to 40-min drive (2-hr cycle) north from the ferry pier at Craignure.

Cycle hire On Yer Bike, Salen, T01680-300501. Daily rental £9, weekly £35. Also has a shop by the ferry terminal in Craignure, T01680-812580.

Ferry To **Oban** from **Craignure**, 5-7 times daily Mon-Sat and 5 times on Sun, 45 mins, £4.90 one way per passenger, £43.50 per car, 5-day return £8.25 and £59, CalMac Oban, T01631-566688, CalMac Craignure, T01680-812343. To **Lochaline** on the Morvern Peninsula from **Fishnish**, Mon-Sat every 45 mins, 9 times on Sun, 15 mins, £2.90 per passenger, £12.80 per car. There are also ferries to **Kilchoan** on the Ardnamurchan Peninsula from **Tobermory**, 7 times daily Mon-Sat and 5 times daily on Sun (May-Aug).

Tobermory *p66, map p66*
Bus There's a bus from **Tobermory** post office to **Dervaig** and **Calgary**, 4 times a day Mon-Fri and twice on Sat, RN Carmichael, T01688-302220.

Cycle hire A Brown and Son Ironmonger, Main St, T01688-302020, bike hire for £15 per day; Tobermory SYHA, Main St, T0870-004 1151.

West coast Mull *p67*
Ferry A small bicycle/passenger-only ferry, makes the 2-min crossing on demand from **Ulva Ferry**, all year for Mon-Fri sailings 0900-1700, Sun sailings Jun-Aug only. From Easter-Sep show signal at the pier to cross. Oct-Easter best to call the ferryman on T01688-400352, or T01688-500241. Note there's no bus to Ulva Ferry. Either cycle or take the bus to **Salen** and jump on a pre-booked bike, see Cycle hire, above.

South Mull *p68*
Ferry To **Iona**, a passenger-only ferry leaves from **Fionnphort** on Mull frequently Mon-Sat 0815-1815, and Sun hourly 0845-1800, 5 mins, £4.50 return, bicycles free. In summer, G MacCormick runs a late (2000) ferry crossing, T01681-700362.

❶ Directory

Mull *p64, map p65*
Banks Clydesdale Bank, Main St, Tobermory, is Mull's only permanent bank. There's also a mobile bank which tours the island.

Coll, Tiree and Colonsay

Just 13 miles long and 4 miles wide, the trickle of visitors who come to explore low-lying, windswept Coll step onto one of the best-kept secrets in Scotland. Here, on lands where the likes of the mysterious Na Sgeulachan standing stone has stood for over 3000 years, tourism remains almost invisible, the 150 islanders enjoying a natural playground where families can picnic on deserted pearl-white beaches with views towards Mull and the Inner Hebrides. Idyllic neighbouring Tiree or Tir-Iodh (land of corn) also boasts stunning beaches caressed by the waters of the Gulf Stream. Statistically one of the sunniest and windiest locations in the UK, Tiree's billiard-flat hinterland teems with rare birdlife and excited wildlife enthusiasts, whilst offshore, windsurfers, surfers and kitesurfers play in towering waves that since the 1980s have earned Tiree the nickname of 'mini-Hawaii' – in 2007 it even hosted a round of the PBA Windsurfing World Cup. Little wonder Tiree now offers a healthy numbers of B&Bs! Colonsay too is remote, tranquil and undemanding; an island brimming with wildlife, flowers and even a miniature mountain range. Like Tiree, Colonsay has also steadily embraced tourism and in particular self-catering accommodation. It may not be the easiest island to reach but clearly its magic has already been discovered.

Coll → *For listings, see pages 81-82. Phone code 01879. www.visitcoll.co.uk.*

The best of Coll's 23 beaches are on the west coast, at **Killunaig**, **Hogh Bay** and **Feall Bay**. The latter is separated from the nearby **Crossapol Bay** by giant sand dunes managed by the RSPB, the islands largest landowner, to protect the resident corncrake population. The **CalMac** ferry from Oban calls in at Coll's only village, **Arinagour**, where half of the island's population live and where you'll find the post office (and bike hire opposite), petrol station, general store, and cosy **Island Café**. There's no public transport but a taxi is available. If it's not too windy, it's best to explore by bike. It's worth taking a walk up **Ben Hogh** (341 ft), the island's highest point, overlooking Hogh Bay on the west coast, to get a terrific view of the island. Tired of beaches? Try some fishing or the nine-hole golf course at Cliad 2 miles west of Arinagour.

Tiree → *For listings, see pages 81-82. Phone code 01879.*

Arriving in Tiree
Getting there and around CalMac car and passenger ferries sail to the island from Oban, via Coll once daily. The **ferry port** ① *T01879-220337*, is at Scarinish. From 0700-1800 (Monday to Saturday) the whole island is covered by a **Ring n' Ride service** ① *T01879-220419*, a bus/taxi service which operates standard fares and is ideal for exploring the island. Pick up a copy of the *Area Transport Guide to Tiree and Coll* from Oban TIC (see page 31). **Tiree Airport** ① *T01879-220309*, where the flight from Glasgow arrives, is at The Reef.

Places in Tiree
Tiree is a low, flat island, only about 11 miles long and 6 miles across at its widest, and is also known by the nickname 'Tir fo Thuinn', or 'Land below the waves'. It is one of the best places to surf in the British Isles. When seen from a distance most of it disappears below the horizon, save its two highest hills, **Ben Hynish** (462 ft) and **Beinn Hough** (390 ft), on the west coast. Though flat, remember that Tiree's fierce winds can make cycling hard work. Campervans laden with surf-gear are a reminder that this is a windsurfing paradise and each October Tiree hosts the week-long **Tiree Wave Classic**. Scores of world-class windsurfers come to compete and party, putting accommodation at a premium.

The ferry port is at **Scarinish**, at the western edge of the sweep of **Gott Bay**. The main village of Scarinish is also where to find the Co-op supermarket, the post office and the bank, there's also a garage at the pier head. About 4 miles from Scarinish, past the delicious locally sourced shellfish and meats served for dinner at the excellent **Elephants End restaurant** above Gott Bay (see Restaurants, page 81), is Vaul Bay, where aside from golf, there are the well-preserved remains of **Dun Mor**, a Pictish Broch built around the first century AD and standing on a rocky outcrop to the west of the bay.

The island's main road runs northwest from Scarinish, past the beautiful beach at **Balephetrish Bay** to **Balevullin**, where you can see some good examples of restored traditional thatched houses. Just to the south, at Sandaig, is the **Sandaig Museum** ① *open all year around, but the summer exhibition is open Jul-Sep, Tue and Sat afternoon*, a thatched croft inside which displays tell of the island's social history.

In the southwestern corner of the island is the spectacular headland of **Ceann a'Mara**, or Kenavara. The massive cliffs are home to thousands of sea birds. East from here, across the golden sands of **Balephuil Bay**, is the island's highest hill, Ben Hynish, topped by a radar-tracking station resembling a giant golf ball. It's worth the climb to the top for the magnificent views over the island and to the distant Outer Hebrides. Below Ben Hynish, to the east, is the village of **Hynish**, where you'll find the **Signal Tower Museum**, which tells the story of the building of the **Skerryvore Lighthouse** (1840-1844) by Alan Stevenson, an uncle of Robert Louis Stevenson. This incredible feat of engineering was carried out from Hynish, where a dry dock/reservoir was built for shipping materials by boat to the Skerryvore reef, 11 miles to the southwest.

Colonsay → *For listings, see pages 81-82. Phone code 01951.*

Arriving in Colonsay

Getting there and around There are ferry sailings from Oban arriving at Scalasaig on the east coast. From Kennacraig and Port Askaig there is one sailing a week on Wednesday. Ferries need to be booked well in advance during the summer months. For those on the island without their own transport, there's a limited bus and postbus service around the island from Monday to Saturday. ▶▶ See Transport, page 82.

Places in Colonsay

Colonsay's population of around 120 lives in the three small villages, the largest of which is **Scalasaig**, the ferry port. A few miles north of the ferry, in the middle of the island, is **Colonsay House**, dating from 1772. It was sold, along with the rest of the island, in 1904 to Lord Strathcona, who had made his fortune in Canada with the Hudson Bay Company and went on to found the Canadian Pacific Railway. The house is not open to the public but the lovely **gardens** ① *Wed and Fri 1200-1700, £2, children £1*, and woods, full of rhododendrons, giant palms and exotic shrubs, are worth a stroll. There's also the chance to buy home-baking and a cup of coffee near the house.

There are several standing stones, the best of which are **Fingal's Limpet Hammers**, at Kilchattan, southwest of Colonsay House. There are also Iron Age forts, such as **Dun Eibhinn**, next to the hotel in Scalasaig. Colonsay is also home to a wide variety of wildlife and over 190 species of birds have apparently been recorded. You can see choughs, one of Britain's rarest birds, as well as corncrakes, buzzards, falcons, merlins and perhaps even the odd golden eagle or sea eagle. There are also otters, seals and wild goats (said to be descended from the survivors of the Spanish Armada ships wrecked in 1588). The jewel in the island's crown, though, lies 6 miles north of Scalasaig, past Colonsay House, at **Kiloran Bay**. The beach here is described as the finest in the Hebrides. Just a glimpse of this magnificent half mile of golden sands, backed by tiers of grassy dunes, with massive breakers rolling in off the Atlantic, is worth the two-hour ferry crossing alone.

Just off the southern tip of Colonsay is the island of **Oronsay**, 2 miles square with a population of six, and one of the highlights of a visit to Colonsay. The name derives from the Norse for 'ebb-tide island', which is a fitting description as Oronsay can be reached on foot at low tide, across the mud flats known as 'The Strand'. It takes about an hour to walk from the south end of Colonsay to the ruins of a 14th-century **Augustinian Priory**. This was home of some of the most highly skilled medieval craftsmen in the Western Highlands. A surviving example of their work is the impressive Oronsay Cross and the beautifully carved tombstones, on display in the **Prior's House**. Make sure you take wellies for the walk across the Strand and check on the tides. Tide tables are available at the hotel or shop. Spring tides (new and full moon) allow about three to four hours to walk across and back, which is just enough time to see the priory but little else. An alternative is to time one way to coincide with the postbus.

Coll, Tiree and Colonsay listings

For hotel and restaurant price codes and other relevant information, see pages 13-20.

⊖ Where to stay

Coll *p79*
£££-££ Coll Hotel, Arinagour, T01879-230334. A comfortable, 6-bedroom family hotel overlooking the village and serving very good food (**££-£**).
££ Caolas House, T01879-230438. A friendly, cosy farmhouse B&B south of Arinagour, by the beach, with terrific home-cooking. Both also available for let.

Tiree *p79*
££ Glebe House, Scarinish, T01879-220758. Comfortable accommodation with sea views across Gott Bay. Also dinner if requested.
££-£ Scarinish Hotel, Scarinish, T01879-220308. Located right by the old harbour, this modest hotel has fabulous views across the bay from its dining area where the simply served local beef, lamb and shellfish will tickle your tastebuds.
£ Mill House Hostel, Cornaigmore, T01879-220435. Fantastic bunkhouse accommodation close to Loch Bhasapol. Bike hire available.

Colonsay *p80*
Accommodation on Colonsay is limited and must be booked well in advance. Even self-catering options are hard to come by, because the same families return year after year. For details on 20 self-catering options see **Colonsay Cottages**, T01951-200312, www.colonsay.org.uk/estate.
£££-££ Isle of Colonsay Hotel, a few hundred yards from the ferry, T01951-200316. A cosy 18th-century inn with 9 rooms, a friendly bar, open fire and excellent food. They also arrange island tours.
££-£ The Hannahs, 4 Uragaig, T01950-200150. 3 rooms. Cosy and friendly, with renowned home-cooking including a

breakfast that will 'blow your socks off'. Also offer ferry pick-up.
£ Colonsay Keeper's Lodge, 2 km from the ferry, T01951-200312, www.colonsay.org.uk. Open all year. A comfortable backpackers' hostel, which sleeps 16. Phone for a lift from the ferry.

⊙ Restaurants

Coll *p79*
££-£ Island Café, Arinagour, T01879-230262. Licensed and great for daytime snacks, coffee and soups. Its Sun lunch is popular, including a roast, shortbread, cheese and oatcakes (from £12.50). Whilst adults dine or laze on the sofas enjoying the sea view, there are toys, books and even table football for the kids.

Tiree *p79*
££ Elephants End, above Gott Bay, T01879-220694. Serves excellent lunches and dinners in a snug restaurant (BYO).
££ The Glassary Restaurant, Sandaig T01879-220684. Mon-Sat 1700-2100. Delicious dinners and Sun lunch.
£ An Talla Café and Gift Shop, Crossapol, T07801-435599. Mon-Sat 1030-1600. Coffees, home-baking and light lunches.
£ The Cobbled Cow, by the airport. Terrific home-baking, good for a snack.

⊙ What to do

Tiree *p79*
Atlantic Trekking, Jane Isaacson, T01879-220881. Pony trekking.
Skipinnish Tours, Skipinnish, Ruaig, www.skipinnish-sea-tours.co.uk, T01879-220009. From £15-40 per person for trips (Apr-Oct) that include shark and whale spotting and trips to Staffa, Lunga and out to Skerryvore Lighhouse (4 hrs).
Tiree Sand Yachts, 16 Crossapol, T01879-220317. Sand yachting.

Wild Diamond Watersports, Burnside Cottage, Cornaig, T07712-159205, www.surfschoolscotland.co.uk. Offers surfing, windsurfing, kitesurfing and kayaking equipment hire and courses.

Colonsay *p80*

For wildlife, archaeological and sightseeing tours of the island by bus or on foot, call T01951-200320. On Wed there's also the chance to do a whistle-stop tour of the island before the ferry departs for Kennacraig, from £10, children £5, www.colonsay.org.uk.

⊖ Transport

Coll *p79*

Cycle hire **An Acarsaid**, Arinagour, T01879-220421. Hires bicycles.

Ferry CalMac, car/passenger ferries leave for **Oban**, daily Fri-Wed, 2 hrs 40 mins, £17.30 return per passenger, £89 per car. The ferry from **Coll** to **Tiree**, 50 mins, costs £5.50 return per passenger, £26.40 per car.

Taxi Barritts, T01879-230402. Taxi service.

Tiree *p79*

Air Tiree has an airport with 1 flight daily Mon-Sat, all year round to **Glasgow**, 45 mins.

Cycle hire **Millhouse Hostel**, Cornaigmore, T01879-220435. Hires bikes.

Ferry CalMac car/passenger ferries sail to **Oban**, via **Coll** once daily, 3 hrs 50 mins, see above under Coll for prices.

Taxi John Kennedy Taxis, T01879-220419. Shared and private taxi hire.

Colonsay *p80*

Cycle hire As the island is only 8 miles long by 3 miles wide, you might consider hiring a bicycle. Bike hire from A McConnel, T01951-200355.

Ferry There are ferry sailings to **Oban**, once daily Mon, Wed, Thu, Fri and Sun, 2 hrs, £22.80 per passenger for 5-day return, £114 per car. To **Kennacraig**, 1 sailing on Wed, 3 hrs 35 mins. To **Port Askaig**, 1 sailing on a Wed, 1 hr 15 mins, £5.10 one way per passenger, £26 per car. Ferries need to be booked well in advance during the summer months (Apr-Sep).

Islay and Jura

Islay (pronounced eye-la), the most southerly of the Hebridean islands and one of the most populous, with around 4000 inhabitants, enjoys a rich farming and crofting heritage but it has one particular claim to fame – single malt whisky. Aside from whisky, people also come here to watch birds. The island is something of an ornithologists' wonderland, and from October to April plays host to migrating barnacle and white-fronted geese flying down from Greenland in their thousands for the winter. The short ferry crossing from Islay takes you to Jura, a primeval and uncompromising place; a lost world, pervaded by an almost haunting silence. The words 'wild' and 'remote' tend to get overused in describing the many Hebridean islands, but in the case of Jura they are, if anything, an understatement. Jura has one road, one hotel, six sporting estates and 5000 red deer, which outnumber the 117 people by 25:1, the human population having been cleared to turn the island into a huge deer forest. Rather appropriately, the name Jura derives from the Norse 'dyr-ey', meaning deer island. Yes, Jura is beautiful – but arguably at a price. For whilst it may be heaven for the landed gentry who control the vast estates, the distinct lack of development ensures affordable housing for the locals remains beyond the grasp of many.

Islay & Jura

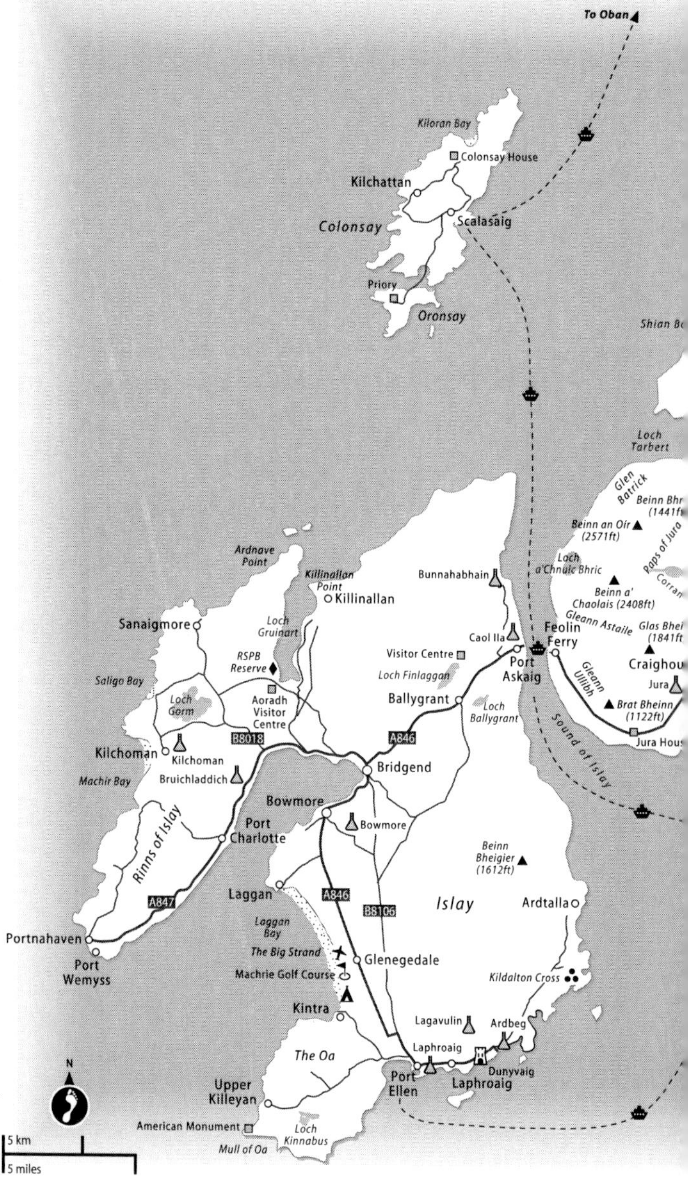
To Oban
Kiloran Bay
Colonsay House
Kilchattan
Scalasaig
Colonsay
Priory
Oronsay
Shian B
Loch Tarbert
Glen Batrick
Beinn Bhr (1441f
Beinn an Oir (2571ft)
Paps of Jura
Loch a'Chnuic Bhric
Beinn a' Chaolais (2408ft)
Corran
Gleann Astaile
Glas Bhei (1841ft
Feolin Ferry
Craighou
Jura
Gleann Ullibh
Brat Bheinn (1122ft)
Jura Hous
Sound of Islay
Ardnave Point
Killinallan Point
Killinallan
Bunnahabhain
Sanaigmore
Loch Gruinart
Caol Ila
RSPB Reserve
Visitor Centre
Port Askaig
Loch Finlaggan
Saligo Bay
Loch Gorm
Aoradh Visitor Centre
Ballygrant
Loch Ballygrant
B8018
A846
Kilchoman
Kilchoman
Bridgend
Machir Bay
Bruichladdich
Bowmore
Bowmore
Port Charlotte
Rinns of Islay
Beinn Bheigier (1612ft)
Laggan
A846
B8106
Islay
Ardtalla
A847
Portnahaven
Laggan Bay
The Big Strand
Port Wemyss
Glenegedale
Machrie Golf Course
Kildalton Cross
Kintra
Lagavulin
Ardbeg
The Oa
Laphroaig
Port Ellen
Dunyvaig
Laphroaig
Upper Killeyan
American Monument
Loch Kinnabus
Mull of Oa
N
5 km
5 miles

Map labels:
Luing
Cruach Scarba (1474ft)
Scarba
Whirlpool
Gulf of Corryvreckan
Glengarrisdale Bay
Kinuachdrach
Kinuachdrach Harbour
Barnhill
Glendebadel Bay
Ben Garrisdale (1198ft)
Corpach Bay
Beinn Bhreac (1533ft)
Ardlussa
Rainberg Mór (1487ft)
To Tayvallich
Jura
Inverlussa
Gleann Aoistail
Keillmore
Lagg
Loch Lesgamaill
Danna Island
Beinn Shiantaidh (2476ft)
Kilmory
Lowlandman's Bay
Leargybreack
Point of Knap
Loch Caolisport
Sound of Jura
Kilberry
Ardpatrick Point
To Kennacraig
Gigha
Ardminish
Sound of Gigha
Tayinloan
Cara Island
Killean
KINTYRE

Islay → *For listings, see pages 90-92.*
Phone code 01496.

In addition to innumerable tea shops, Islay offers the unique opportunity to visit several of Scotland's most impressive distilleries in one day. The island has eight working distilleries in total (see box, page 87) and their distinctive peaty malts are considered to be among the finest. At the end of May each year, the island hosts the **Islay Malt and Music Festival** for which the distillers produce their special edition malts (see Festivals, page 91).

Arriving in Islay
Getting there and around The airport is at Glenegedale, a few miles north of Port Ellen on the road to Bowmore. The ferry from Kennacraig to Port Ellen sails twice daily on Mondays, Tuesdays, Thursdays, Fridays and Saturdays and once on Wednesdays and Sundays. A ferry also sails from Kennacraig to Port Askaig once daily on Monday, Wednesday and Friday. The ferry from Oban to Port Askaig sails on Wednesdays. For those without their own transport, there's a regular bus service around Islay, with **Islay Coaches** ① *T01496-840273*. There are buses from Portnahaven to Port Ellen, via Port Charlotte, Bridgend, Bowmore and the airport; from Port Askaig to Port Ellen via Ballygrant, Bridgend, Bowmore and the airport; from Port Ellen to Ardbeg, Bowmore, Port Askaig and Portnahaven; and also a postbus to Bunnahabhain. Buses run regularly from Monday to Saturday, but only once on Sunday. → *See Transport, page 91.*

Tourist information Islay TIC ① *Bowmore, T01496-810254, Apr-Sep Mon-Sat 1000-1700, Sun 1400-1700, Oct-Mar Mon-Fri 1000-1600*, will find accommodation for you. Islay can be reached by air from Glasgow (for details, see page 7).

Port Ellen and around

Port Ellen is the largest place on Islay and the main ferry port, yet it still has the feel of a sleepy village. There are many day trips from Port Ellen. A road runs east out to **Ardtalla**, where it ends. Along the way, it passes three distilleries, first **Laphroaig**, then **Lagavulin** and lastly **Ardbeg**, all of which offer guided tours, see box, opposite. Between the Lagavulin and Ardbeg distilleries is the dramatically sited 16th-century ruin of **Dunyvaig Castle**, once the main naval base and fortress of the Lords of the Isles. Five miles further on is the impressive **Kildalton Cross**, standing in the graveyard of the ruined 13th-century chapel. The eighth-century cross is well preserved and is one of Scotland's most important Early Christian monuments, and the carvings depict biblical scenes.

Southwest of Port Ellen a road runs out to a small, rounded peninsula known as **The Oa**, an area of varied beauty, both wild and pastoral, and with a wonderful coastline. The road runs as far as **Upper Killeyan**, from where it's about a mile uphill to the spectacular headland at the **Mull of Oa**. Here you'll see the strange-looking **American monument**. The obelisk commemorates the shipwrecks offshore of two US ships, the *Tuscania* and the *Ontranto*, both of which sank in 1918 at the end of the First World War. There's a great walk north from the Mull of Oa up to Kintra, but it's best to start out from Kintra.

A turn-off from the road to The Oa leads north to **Kintra**, at the south end of The Big Strand at Laggan Bay, with 5 miles of sands and dunes. There's a restaurant and accommodation here, and it's a great place for camping. The restaurant is at the end of the road, with the beach on one side and, on the other, a wild and spectacular coastal walk incorporating caves and the impressive **Soldier's Rock** sea-stack. Ask at the TIC for the *Explore Islay* walking trail leaflet. Just to the north of Kintra is the **Machrie golf course**, a golfing experience not to be missed.

Bowmore and the Rinns of Islay

The A846 runs north from Port Ellen, straight as a pool cue, to Bowmore, the island's administrative capital and second largest village. Founded in 1768 by the Campbells, it retains a sleepy air. The village is laid out in a grid plan with the main street running straight up the hill from the pier to the unusual round church, designed to ward off evil spirits, who can hide only in corners. Thankfully, the good spirit stayed behind and can be found at the **Bowmore Distillery**, just to the west of Main Street. This is the oldest of the island's distilleries, founded in 1779.

North of Bowmore, **Bridgend**, is the site of the tiny **Islay Ales Brewery**. Here too the A846 joins the A847 which runs west to the hammerhead peninsula known as the **Rinns of Islay** (*rinns* is derived from the Gaelic for promontory). A few miles west of Bridgend the B8017 turns north to the **RSPB Reserve** at **Loch Gruinart**. The mudflats and fields at the head of the loch provide winter grazing for huge flocks of barnacle and white-fronted geese from Greenland, arriving in late October. There's an excellent RSPB visitor centre at **Aoradh** (pronounced *oorig*), which houses an observation point with telescopes and CCTV, and there's a hide across the road. There are about 110 species of bird breeding on Islay, including the rare chough and corncrake.

The coastal scenery around the Rinns is very impressive, particularly at **Killinallan Point**, a beautiful and lonely headland at the far northeast of Loch Gruinart. Also impressive is **Ardnave Point**, west of Loch Gruinart, and further west along the north coast, **Sanaigmore**. The best beaches are at **Saligo** and **Machir Bay** on the west coast, past Loch Gorm. Both are lovely, wide, golden beaches backed by high dunes but swimming is ill-advised due to dangerous undercurrents. Less than a mile behind Machir

Islay's malts distilled

Ardbeg, T01496-302244, www.ardbeg. com, hourly tours Sep-May Mon-Fri 1000-1600, Jun-Aug daily 1000-1700, £3. Describes itself as the peatiest malt whisky in the world. This may be a robust and powerful malt but in 1981 all operations were sadly mothballed. In 1997 it was bought by Glenmorangie and reopened to ensure the malt first distilled in 1815 continued to flow from within the white-washed walls on Islay's eastern shoreline.

Bowmore, T01496-558 9011, www. bowmore.com, mid-Sep to Easter Mon-Fri 0900-1700, Sat 0900-1200, tours Mon-Fri 1000, 1100, 1400, 1500, Sat 1000, £4, concessions £2. Bowmore is the oldest distillery on Islay. Its flagship is the 12-year-old single malt. The Craftsman's Tour (£22) is highly recommended and offers the chance to savour many a single malt during an informative tour behind the scenes. Established in 1779, It has visitor centre with additional information on the history of the distillery and also rents luxuriously appointed former workers cottages just yards from the shore and distillery. Call for details.

Bruichladdich, T01496-850190, www.bruichladdich.com, Mon-Fri 0900-1700, Sat 1000-1600, 45-min tours Oct-Easter Mon-Fri 1130 and 1430, Sat 1130, Easter-Sep additional tour 1030. Mon-Fri 1030, 1130, 1430, Sat 1030 and 1430 only, £5 including dram. Produces a range of innovative malts including Mood Malts, Multi-Vintage and Single Vintage. Claims to produce different Bruichladdich's by drawing upon its maturing stocks that date back to 1964 (pronounced 'brook-laddie').

Bunnahabhain, T01496-840646, www. bunnahabhain.co.uk, Easter-Oct Mon-Fri, tours 1030, 1400, 1515, winter tours by appointment only, you are strongly advised to call ahead to double check all tour times and distillery opening hours. Started in 1881 (and pronounced 'bun-a-havan'), this is known as the 'gentle giant' of Islay because it's the least peaty of the Islay malts. The distiller produces a 12-, 18- and 25-year-old malt and also a 34-year-old malt.

Caol Ila, T01496-302760, www.discovering-distilleries.com, Apr-Oct Mon-Fri 0915-1600, tours 0930, 1045, 1345, 1500, £5. Pronounced 'coal-eela', this distillery was founded in 1846 and lies close to Port Askaig, with great views across the Sound of Islay to Jura. Unlike most of its island peers, this single malt is best before dinner.

Kilchoman, Rockside Farm, Bruichladdich, T01496-850011, www.kilchomandistillery. com, visitor centre open Apr-Oct Mon-Sat 1000-1700, Nov-Mar Mon-Fri 1000-1700. Islay's newest distillery (established 2005). It already produces almost 100,000 litres of alcohol per year. Kilchoman claims to be one of only half-a-dozen distilleries in Scotland that carries out traditional floor maltings. All its barley is grown in the fields next door.

Lagavulin, T01496-302730, www. discovering-distilleries.com/lagavulin, tours Mon-Fri by appointment only at 1000, 1130, 1430, £5. Their 16-year-old single malt is one of the classics and also makes the ideal after-dinner tipple. A very interesting tour.

Laphroaig, T01496-302418, www. laphroaig.com, tours all year by appointment only 1015 and 1415, free. The closest to Port Ellen, and its wonderful setting is summed up by its name, meaning 'The beautiful hollow by the broad bay' in Gaelic. According to many this is the ultimate in malt whisky and is at its best after dinner. This distillery has a reputation for one of the best whisky tours on Islay.

Bay you'll also find **Kilchoman Distillery and Visitor Centre** ① *T01496-850011, Mon-Fri Nov-Mar, Apr-Oct Mon-Sat 1000-1700, tours 1100 and 1500*, the isle's newest working distiller of the water of life. If you fancy a canter along the sands, this is also where to find the **Rockside Farm Trekking Centre** ① *T01496-850231*.

Port Charlotte is without doubt the most charming of Islay's villages, with rows of well-kept, whitewashed cottages stretched along the wide bay. Here, below the comfortable youth hostel is the **Islay Natural History Trust** ① *T01496-850288, Easter-Oct, Mon-Fri 1000-1600, Jun-Aug Mon-Sat 1000-1600, £3, concessions £2, children £1.50. All tickets are valid for a week*. It's a must for anyone interested in flora and fauna, with good displays on geology and natural history, a video room and reference library. Housed 300 yds away in a former Free Church, the compact **Museum of Islay Life** ① *T01496-850358, Easter-Oct open every day 1000-1630, £3, concessions £2, children £1*, is especially worth a visit with photographs and over 1600 exhibits, including an illicit still found on the island, highlighting the rich past and culture of the native Ileach's (*ee-lach's*). Close-by there's bike hire, whilst just south of the village you'll find the pleasant **Port Mor Campsite** and **Bon Appetit Café** (T01496-850441). At the southern end of the Rinns, 7 miles south of Port Charlotte, is the picturesque fishing and crofting village of Portnahaven, its Hebridean cottages rising steeply above the deeply indented harbour and where the cosy **An Tigh Seinsse bar** by the harbour serves delicious meals including Queen scallops and mains of Islay beef.

Port Askaig and around

Port Askaig is Islay's other ferry port, with connections to the mainland and to the islands of Jura and Colonsay. It's little more than a dock, a car park and a pub huddled at the foot of a steep, wooded hillside. A short walk north along the coast is the **Caol Ila Distillery**, and a couple of miles further north, at the end of the road which branches left before you enter Port Askaig, is the beautifully situated **Bunnahabhain Distillery**.

The A846 runs east from Bridgend out to Port Askaig passing through **Ballygrant**, just to the south of **Loch Finlaggan**. Here, on two *crannogs* (artificial islands), were the headquarters of the Lords of the Isles, the ancestors of Clan Donald. The MacDonalds ruled from Islay for nearly 350 years, over a vast area covering all of the islands off the west coast and almost the whole of the western seaboard from Cape Wrath to the Mull of Kintyre. To the northeast of the loch, there's the **Finlaggan Centre** ① *T01496-810629, Apr-Sep Mon-Sat 1030-1630, Sun 1300-1630, £3, concessions £2, children £1*, which has been expanded to accommodate more objects from the ancient site. You can walk across the fen to **Eilean Mor**, where you'll find a medieval chapel and several ornately carved gravestones. On neighbouring, **Eilean na Comhairle** (The Council of the Isle) the Lords of the Isles decided policy.

Jura ➜ *For listings, see pages 90-92.*

Arriving in Jura ➜ *Phone code 01496.*
Getting there and around A small car and passenger ferry makes the regular five-minute crossing daily to Port Askaig on Islay. For times, contact **Argyll & Bute Council** ① *T01496-840681*. There's also a handy passenger-only ferry between Tayvallich and Craighouse that runs from June to the end of September. There is a bus service on Jura, which runs from Feolin Ferry to Craighouse several times a day, Monday to Saturday. A few buses continue to Lagg and Inverlussa and return to Craighouse. Note that some journeys are by request

only and must be booked the day before. Contact **Alex Dunnichie** ① *T01496-820314*. Alternatively, hire a bike. ▸▸ *See Transport, page 91.*

Places in Jura
Three things bring people to sparsely populated Jura, where in early August locals and visitors participate in the open water rowing competitions of the grandly titled Jura Regatta. First there's the scenery. This is one of the last, true wildernesses in the British Isles and perfect for some real off-the-beaten-track walking. The appealingly named **Paps of Jura**, are three breast-shaped peaks that dominate not only the island itself but also the view for miles around. From Kintyre, Mull, Coll and Tiree, and from the mountains of mainland Scotland from Skye to Arran, they can be seen on the horizon. The Paps provide some tough hillwalking and require good navigational skills, or a guide. It takes a good eight hours to cover all three peaks, though during the Paps of Jura fell race they are covered in just three hours. A good place to start is by the three-arch bridge over the Corran River, north of Leargybreack. The first pap you reach is **Beinn a'Chaolais** (2408 ft), next is the highest, **Beinn an Oír** (2571 ft) and the third is **Beinn Shiantaidh** (2476 ft). To find out about guides, ask at **Jura Stores** (T01496-820231) in Craighouse that has provided much needed provisions since the 1890s.

Next there's wildlife. Aside from the thousands of red deer, there are sea eagles and golden eagles in the skies above and the surrounding seas are full of seals, dolphins and porpoises, with the elusive otter making an occasional appearance. And finally, there's whisky. The island's only road leads from the ferry to the only village, Craighouse, 8 miles away on the southeast coast. Here you'll find the **Jura Distillery** ① *T01496-820240, www. isleofjura.com, open all year, tours by appointment, free*, which produces 1½ million litres annually and offers a snifter of the stuff at the end of a friendly and informative tour.

Another of the island's draws is the **Corryvreckan whirlpool** at the very northern tip, between Jura and the uninhabited island of **Scarba**. The notorious whirlpool, the second largest in the world, is in fact a tidal race that creates an action like a gigantic washing machine. It is seen at its awesome best during spring tides, especially with a westerly gale, when this most treacherous stretch of water creates oar falls of 25 ft and the terrible roar can be heard for up to 10 miles away. A two-hour tidal difference between the sound on the east and the Atlantic flood tides combine with the gulf of Corryvreckan's steep sides and underwater pinnacle, the Hag, to create the vortex. The Royal Navy officially says it's unsailable, but that doesn't stop several local boat tours actually going over the top of it. It is named after a Viking, Bhreacan, who anchored his boat here for three days and nights with a rope woven from the hair of virgins. Unsurprisingly, the rope parted under the strain, casting doubt on the status of one of the contributors, and Bhreacan drowned. To get there, follow the rough track from **Ardlussa** to **Kinuachdrach**, or get someone to drive you, then it's a 2-mile walk. Before setting out, ask at the hotel for information and directions.

In 1947, the Corryvreckan nearly claimed the life of one Eric Arthur Blair – aka George Orwell – who had come to Jura to finish the novel that would later become *Nineteen Eighty-Four*. Despite being diagnosed with TB, Orwell went to live on Jura with his three-year-old adopted son, Richard, in spartan conditions at **Barnhill**, a cottage in the middle of nowhere and 25 miles from the nearest doctor. That summer he invited his niece and nephew to stay, and one day took them out into the Corryvrekan in a tiny boat. When the outboard motor was ripped off by the force of the tide and the boat capsized, Orwell and the others only just escaped with their lives by clambering onto a small island; they were later rescued by a passing lobster boat. Today, Barnhill attracts literary pilgrims and, though closed to the public, can be rented for a week's stay (see Where to stay, below).

Also on the island, 3 miles south of Craighouse village, at Ardfin, is the beautiful **walled garden** ① *daily 0900-1700, £2.50*, at Jura House, which is filled with wild flowers and Australasian plants and trees. There's also a tea tent open in summer and plenty of good walks through the surrounding woods or down to the nearby beaches. See Where to stay, below, for details of self-catering accommodation in Jura House.

Islay and Jura listings

For hotel and restaurant price codes and other relevant information, see pages 13-20.

⊝ Where to stay

Islay *p85, map p84*
£££ Glenegedale, Port Ellen, T01496-300400, www.glenegedalehouse.com. 5 rooms. The owner of this guesthouse has every right to boast about her breakfasts – in 2006 at another island address she won the Best Breakfast in Britain Award. She's taken the same recipe for success to her new place, which offers a peat fire and the chance for guests to enjoy nature and distillery tours.
£££ Harbour Inn, Main St, Bowmore, just yards from the shore, T01496-810330, www.harbour-inn.com. 7 tastefully furnished en suite bedrooms, but the real treat is the fabulous restaurant complete with cosy bar (see Restaurants, below).
£££ Kilmeny Country House, Ballygrant, 4 miles from Port Askaig, T01496-840668, www.kilmeny.co.uk. With wonderful views, this is a stylish rural option with 4 comfortable rooms and highly rated food (dinner £36). Serves locally caught shellfish and reared beef in a friendly atmosphere. Recommended.
£££-££ Port Charlotte Hotel, on the seafront, Port Charlotte, T01496-850360. 10 rooms. Restored Victorian inn with gardens and conservatory, serving good food (see Restaurants, below). One of the best around.
££ Sornbank, Bridgend, T01496-810544, www.sornbank.co.uk. B&B close to amenities, with excellent breakfast.

Lets 2 self-contained flats on a weekly or fortnightly basis.
£ Port Charlotte Youth Hostel, Port Charlotte, T01496 850385. Open Apr-Oct. Highly recommended, this very comfortable, spacious hostel is close to the ales, malts and tasty meals served by the **Port Charlotte Hotel** and **Lochindaal Hotel**.

Self-catering
Coull Farm Cottage, Bruichladdich, T01496-850317. Sleeps 5 in a cosy cottage with panoramic views and excellent nearby walks. From £200 per week.
Drumlanrig, Carnduncan, Gruinart, T01496-850503. Sleeps 1-6 people in a well equipped and byre cottage and farmhouse cottage, located close to the renowned RSPB bird-spotting reserve and handy for the likes of beaches and pony trekking. From £250-550 per week.

Jura *p88, map p84*
£££-££ Jura Hotel, Craighouse, T01496-820243, www.jurahotel.co.uk. Open all year. 18 bedrooms. The island's one and only hotel, overlooking the Small Isles Bay. The hotel bar is the island's social hub, and hosts Steve and Fiona Walton, who have been here for 25 years, can provide information on walks as well as arranging tours to the Corryvreckan and fishing trips. The restaurant serves good food, see Restaurants, below. Great place to relax after a hike and enjoy banter with the locals. Gets very busy in summer. Camping is also possible in the hotel grounds.
££ The Manse, Craighouse, T01496-820384. Friendly, 3-bedroom option in the village.

£ Kinuachdrachd Farm and Bunkhouse, T07899-912116. Located to the north of the island. Friendly, comfortable B&B (sleeps 4) and bunkhouse (sleeps 6) run by Mike Richardson. Also offers wildlife tours.

Self-catering

Barnhill, contact Kate Johnson, T01786-850274. Sleeps 7. Very remote – 14 miles north of the nearest pub and shop. For more ascetic souls, and devotees of George Orwell. From £550 per week.

Jura House, contact Mirjam Cool in Craighouse, T01496-820315, mirjamcool@aol.com. Sleeps up to 15. At the top end of the comfort scale. £900-1400 per week.

Jura Lodge, T01496-820240, www.isleofjura.com. The most salubrious choice. Housed inside the distillery grounds, the refurbished lodge is available for private use at certain times of the year. It sleeps up to 8. They also run residential whisky appreciation courses. From £1500 for the week.

Restaurants

Islay p85, map p84

£££ Harbour Inn, Main St, Bowmore, T01496-810330, www.harbour-inn.com. Serves outstanding seafood in a stylish setting.

£££ Kilmeny Country House, Ballygrant, 4 miles from Port Askaig, T01496-840668, www.kilmeny.co.uk. Serves locally caught shellfish and reared beef in a friendly atmosphere. Highly rated food, recommended.

£££-££ Port Charlotte Hotel, on the seafront, Port Charlotte, T01496-850360. Serves tasty, locally sourced dishes.

££-£ Lochindaal Hotel, Port Charlotte T01496-850202. You'll find locally caught shellfish, including mussels and scallops on the menu, and beef or lamb sourced from Hebridean farms.

Jura p88, map p84

££-£ Jura Hotel, see Where to stay, above. Currently the only option for either a

bar meal or evening dining. Try the fresh langoustines or famed venison pie.

Festivals

Islay p85, map p84

May Islay Festival of Malt and Music, www.feisile.org. Annual folk music festival, for which the distillers produce their own special edition malts.

Sep Islay Jazz Festival, www.islayjazzfestival.co.uk.

Jura p88, map p84

Aug Jura Regatta.

What to do

Jura p88, map p84

Islay Birding, The Old Byre Main St, Port Charlotte, contact Jeremy Hastings, T01496-850010, www.islaybirding.co.uk. Discover the nature of Islay with Jeremy on his award-winning dawn or dusk, £30; ½-day and £60 day wildlife safaris. Recommended.

Mike Richardson, T07899-912116. Guides hill walks and Orwell trails (Easter-Oct) from £30 per person (minimum charge of £75 if fewer than 3 people) and runs a landrover taxi service on Jura.

Transport

Islay p85, map p84

Cycle hire Mountain Bike Hire, 33 Main St, Port Charlotte, T01496-850488. Bike hire available for £10 per day.

Ferry CalMac offices in Kennacraig, T01880-730253, and Port Ellen, T01496-302209, £16.25 per passenger for 5-day return, £88 per car. **Kennacraig** from **Port Askaig**, once daily Mon, Wed, Fri. To **Oban** from Port Askaig, Wed, 4 hrs 15 mins, £13.75 per passenger, £68 per car. To **Colonsay** from Port Askaig, Wed.

Jura *88, map p84*
Cycle hire Jura Bike Hire, Keils, just beyond Craighouse, T07092-180747.

Ferry A small car and passenger ferry makes the regular 5-min crossing daily to **Port Askaig** on Islay, £2.50 return per passenger, £14 per car, **Feolin Ferry**. For times, **Argyll & Bute Council**, T01496-840681. There's also a handy passenger-only ferry between **Craighouse** to the mainland, **Tayvallich** (off B841), that runs Jun-Sep, £15 one-way with bus connections.

Contents

Footnotes

Index

Titles available in the Footprint *Focus* range

Latin America	UK RRP	US RRP
Bahia & Salvador	£7.99	$11.95
Brazilian Amazon	£7.99	$11.95
Brazilian Pantanal	£6.99	$9.95
Buenos Aires & Pampas	£7.99	$11.95
Cartagena & Caribbean Coast	£7.99	$11.95
Costa Rica	£8.99	$12.95
Cuzco, La Paz & Lake Titicaca	£8.99	$12.95
El Salvador	£5.99	$8.95
Guadalajara & Pacific Coast	£6.99	$9.95
Guatemala	£8.99	$12.95
Guyana, Guyane & Suriname	£5.99	$8.95
Havana	£6.99	$9.95
Honduras	£7.99	$11.95
Nicaragua	£7.99	$11.95
Northeast Argentina & Uruguay	£8.99	$12.95
Paraguay	£5.99	$8.95
Quito & Galápagos Islands	£7.99	$11.95
Recife & Northeast Brazil	£7.99	$11.95
Rio de Janeiro	£8.99	$12.95
São Paulo	£5.99	$8.95
Uruguay	£6.99	$9.95
Venezuela	£8.99	$12.95
Yucatán Peninsula	£6.99	$9.95

Asia	UK RRP	US RRP
Angkor Wat	£5.99	$8.95
Bali & Lombok	£8.99	$12.95
Chennai & Tamil Nadu	£8.99	$12.95
Chiang Mai & Northern Thailand	£7.99	$11.95
Goa	£6.99	$9.95
Gulf of Thailand	£8.99	$12.95
Hanoi & Northern Vietnam	£8.99	$12.95
Ho Chi Minh City & Mekong Delta	£7.99	$11.95
Java	£7.99	$11.95
Kerala	£7.99	$11.95
Kolkata & West Bengal	£5.99	$8.95
Mumbai & Gujarat	£8.99	$12.95

Africa & Middle East	UK RRP	US RRP
Beirut	£6.99	$9.95
Cairo & Nile Delta	£8.99	$12.95
Damascus	£5.99	$8.95
Durban & KwaZulu Natal	£8.99	$12.95
Fès & Northern Morocco	£8.99	$12.95
Jerusalem	£8.99	$12.95
Johannesburg & Kruger National Park	£7.99	$11.95
Kenya's Beaches	£8.99	$12.95
Kilimanjaro & Northern Tanzania	£8.99	$12.95
Luxor to Aswan	£8.99	$12.95
Nairobi & Rift Valley	£7.99	$11.95
Red Sea & Sinai	£7.99	$11.95
Zanzibar & Pemba	£7.99	$11.95

Europe	UK RRP	US RRP
Bilbao & Basque Region	£6.99	$9.95
Brittany West Coast	£7.99	$11.95
Cádiz & Costa de la Luz	£6.99	$9.95
Granada & Sierra Nevada	£6.99	$9.95
Languedoc: Carcassonne to Montpellier	£7.99	$11.95
Málaga	£5.99	$8.95
Marseille & Western Provence	£7.99	$11.95
Orkney & Shetland Islands	£5.99	$8.95
Santander & Picos de Europa	£7.99	$11.95
Sardinia: Alghero & the North	£7.99	$11.95
Sardinia: Cagliari & the South	£7.99	$11.95
Seville	£5.99	$8.95
Sicily: Palermo & the Northwest	£7.99	$11.95
Sicily: Catania & the Southeast	£7.99	$11.95
Siena & Southern Tuscany	£7.99	$11.95
Sorrento, Capri & Amalfi Coast	£6.99	$9.95
Skye & Outer Hebrides	£6.99	$9.95
Verona & Lake Garda	£7.99	$11.95

North America	UK RRP	US RRP
Vancouver & Rockies	£8.99	$12.95

Australasia	UK RRP	US RRP
Brisbane & Queensland	£8.99	$12.95
Perth	£7.99	$11.95

For the latest books, e-books and a wealth of travel information, visit us at:
www.footprinttravelguides.com.

Join us on facebook for the latest travel news, product releases, offers and amazing competitions:
www.facebook.com/footprintbooks.